The Way of a Child

The Way of a Child

AN INTRODUCTION TO THE WORK
OF RUDOLF STEINER FOR CHILDREN

By
A. C. HARWOOD

RUDOLF STEINER PRESS
LONDON

First Impression, 1940
Reprinted, 1940
Second and Revised Edition, 1942
Reprinted, 1945
Third and Revised Edition, 1952
Fourth and Revised Edition, 1967
Second Impression, 1974

© Rudolf Steiner Press 1967

ISBN 0 85440 182 2

MADE AND PRINTED IN GREAT BRITAIN BY
THE GARDEN CITY PRESS LIMITED
LETCHWORTH, HERTFORDSHIRE

PREFACE

This little book is entirely based on the study of Rudolf Steiner's books and lectures on childhood and education, and on many years' experience as a teacher in a school founded to carry out his ideas. I have not endeavoured to distinguish between what is immediately contained in his own works and anything that my own thought and experience may have taught me, or that I may have added by way of illustration. Rather have I tried (as I think he would have wished) to present in my own way that limited part of his work which I feel I have best understood and made my own. A list of such of his own works on education as are translated into English will be found at the end of the book.

I found in writing that the subject matter did not allow that any one theme should be confined to a single chapter: but a theme which had been introduced in one chapter had often to be approached from new points of view in succeeding chapters. I hope that repetition of a theme will always be found to have carried the matter further.

A. C. H.

CONTENTS

                                                                    PAGE

CHAPTER I.—THE PHYSICAL BASIS OF
SPIRITUAL LIFE   9

CHAPTER II.—THE CHILD'S RELATION TO
THE THREEFOLD ORGANISM AND THE
THREEFOLD POWERS OF THE SOUL ...   21

CHAPTER III.—CONSCIOUS POWERS AND
ORGANIC ACTIVITY   36

CHAPTER IV.—THE HEART OF CHILDHOOD   48

CHAPTER V.—LIFE FORCES AND DEATH
FORCES   69

CHAPTER VI.—THE BIRTH OF THE EGO ...   82

CHAPTER VII.—BETWEEN THE INDIVIDUAL
AND THE GENERAL—THE TEMPERA-
MENTS   92

CHAPTER VIII.—THE FORM OF A SCHOOL   105

CHAPTER IX.—EDUCATION AND SOCIETY...   122

NOTE ON THE COVER PICTURE   143

CONTENTS

CHAPTER I.—THE PRIMROSE PATH 9

CHAPTER II.—THE CHILD, HIS BIRTH ... ...

CHAPTER III.—GOVERNING BODIES ...

CHAPTER IV.—... FIELD ... ...

CHAPTER V.—... ... ...

CHAPTER VI.—... ... ...

CHAPTER VII.—... ... ...

CHAPTER VIII.—... ... ...

... NOTES ON ... ...

THE PHYSICAL BASIS OF SPIRITUAL LIFE

It is a right instinct among children to wish to be grown up. Healthy children do not desire to stay with Peter Pan in the garden of childhood, but long for that freedom of their powers which they feel will come to them when they reach the distant and hardly conceivable land of manhood. The instinct is a right one because childhood has only meaning or beauty in that it is a preparation for a different state. Its charm is that it stays only for a moment: its importance is that it will not return. It matters very much that children should be helped to win from childhood all the qualities which it has to give; but no one will be able to help them to do so who is uncertain of the goal towards which childhood is striving, because he has not formed a clear picture of the powers of the fully grown man.

Anyone who reflects upon the powers of his mind or soul will soon discover that he has the capacity of expressing himself in three different worlds, the world of *thinking*, the world of *feeling*, and the world of *willing*. There are many kinds of thinking, from the colourless pure logical thought of geometrical proof to the rich pictures of imagination; there are many types of feeling, ranging from those feelings which are not much more than bodily sensations to the highest spiritual experiences of ecstasy and devotion; there are many degrees of the will, from the half instinctive impulse to the conscious deliberate act: but all forms of human consciousness and activity in their incredible variety can ultimately be referred to one or other, or in part to one and in part to another, of these three different worlds of experience. Like night and day and the seasons of the year, they are archetypal, and the study of the powers of the human soul must begin with them.

That there is a real distinction between these three worlds of experience will become apparent to anyone who studies their various characteristics. Thinking is in every respect the polar opposite of willing. The former is the most conscious of all our activities; not only are we conscious when we think, but we can afterwards think over our thoughts and become conscious of the process of thinking itself. The will on the other hand is the least conscious of our powers; when we move an arm we are quite unconscious of the magical process by which we proceed from the thought ' I will move my arm ' to the movement itself: still less can the will add consciousness to the will which is already willed. We can indeed compare our experiences in thinking and willing to the two states of waking and sleeping. We do not merely pass in daily alternation from sleeping to waking, but in our waking life itself we remain in one part of our experience—in our life of will—asleep.

Between these two opposites, however, there is the third element in human experience; the power of feeling, which in respect of consciousness mediates between the conscious thinking and the unconscious will. In feeling we dream. We have the sense of the beautiful, for example, long before we try by the science of æsthetics to become fully awake to what the beautiful is; whereas a thought cannot truly be said to exist for us until we hold it clearly in our consciousness. Our feelings are indeed often the most potent force in our lives, but it is not easy to be entirely conscious of the very feeling which directs our actions. There is therefore present in us also the third element of experience which dreams. Dreaming not only occurs as an intermediate state between the act of waking and the act of sleeping, or vice versa; it is present as well in our waking life. In each moment of our daily life, waking, dreaming and sleeping are united in the experience of thought, feeling, and will.

The proof of this relation between thinking, feeling and willing need not depend only on purely formal considerations. Everyone knows in concrete flesh and blood the three types of men who live more deeply in the experience of one or other of these three powers. The man whose skill lies in some activity of the will, the craftsman for example, astonishes the intellectual spectator with his inability to bring to consciousness and explain *how* the process is done. He seems to do and not to know what he does. So far from being necessary to skilful action in a craft, consciousness seems even inimical to it. Mukerji* relates that a team of Indian weavers entirely lost their capacity to weave when a Western observer made them conscious of their actual movements. The man of feeling, the artist or poet, too, lives in a dream world of his own. His dreams may or may not be more valuable than the limited but wholly conscious experience of the intellectual— the scientist, for example—but the difference between the two minds and the way this difference expresses itself in conduct will be familiar to everyone.

Parallel with this contrast between thinking, feeling and willing in the matter of consciousness, are many other characteristic differences. Thinking brings the thinker to rest, stopping him even in the midst of action; willing creates movement, commonly actual external movement which is distinctly perceptible; while feeling creates that movement which is at once motion and rest, which moves without tiring, which allays while it excites—the movement of rhythm. All artistic work is rhythmical, all work into which rhythm enters becomes in a measure artistic. Or, to take a further polarity, the act of will is something which essentially goes towards the future—you cannot will into the past. Thinking on the other hand is bound by its very nature to the past. Not that we never think about the future, but when we do

* Caste and Outcast.

so think it is in terms of the past—if we could really think futurity we should all be prophets. The experience of feeling on the other hand is essentially that of the present. The man of feeling 'kisses the joy as it flies,' he has the art by which the thing he is doing *now* seems the most important thing in the world. Happy is the man who has this art at his command.

Much more could be said to develop this theme of the polarity of thinking and willing with feeling as the mediator between them, but an outline sketch of this relationship is perhaps all that is necessary before a further question is raised. For we must now ask, What, if any, is the connection of these powers of the soul with the human body? And is this connection a real one or is it merely a parallelism such as is imagined by some modern psychologies?

It is characteristic of modern science, which eliminates feeling from the field of knowledge, that it has a fairly clear understanding of the connection of conscious thinking processes with the brain and nervous system; but that it has no physical basis for the powers of feeling and willing. The so called 'motor' nerves which are supposed to carry the will, are in reality no more than the bearers of that relatively, small amount of consciousness necessary to every act of will.* If we are not conscious to some degree of a finger, we cannot move it. But the being conscious and the moving are entirely different processes. This inability to find a basis

* Some leading neurologists now recognise that the old conception of 'motor' nerves is untenable.

for feeling and will is perhaps natural with a method of science which denies feeling and will any place in the field of knowledge. In a Spiritual Science however, feeling and will (though in an enhanced condition) have also a vital contribution to make towards knowledge, it is therefore equally natural that in such a science there should appear a living relationship between bodily functions and these two powers of the soul. This relationship is again something which everyone can verify for himself by his own experience and observation. For the same polarity which appears between thinking and willing, considered in their pure spiritual nature, is reflected in the systems of the human body which support them; and the bodily basis of feeling appears, like the feeling itself, in the position of mediator between the other two.

The physical basis of thinking is the system of the head together with the nerves which radiate into every part of the body. It is characteristic of the head that it must be kept as far as possible from the effects of movement. When a man walks, or jumps, the shock of the movement is almost entirely prevented from reaching the head and brain. We have only to knock our head slightly to realise how important it is for the head that the shock of the foot on the ground is broken by the elasticity of our joints before it reaches the brain. The head is a true picture of the still quietness which we need in order to develop our thoughts. Equally characteristic of the brain substance is its lifeless nature. It has been called 'the machine with no moving

14

parts.' The nerve substance must always be fed; in its own nature it is always trying to harden or decay; it is the representative of death in the human being.

But there is a system in the human body which possesses characteristics which are the opposite of this motionless lifeless entity. Like the latter, this system also penetrates the entire human being (systems are not, like organs, mutually exclusive), and wherever it penetrates it brings effects contrary to those of the head and nerves. This is the system of movement manifesting itself externally in the movements of the limbs, and internally in the whole process of digestion and metabolism. But this system is not merely organic; it has also a spiritual function, being, in effect, the physical basis for the power of willing. People of strong will almost invariably move their limbs with energy and decision. When they walk they leave their impress on the ground; when they talk the movements of the jaw (which is the limb in the head) or of the accompanying arms betoken the same liveliness in the system of movement. In children this can be specially clearly observed. The child who walks strongly on his heels, stamping on the ground as though he wanted to leave the imprint of his foot there like Man Friday's, will undoubtedly be a child of strong will, probably of the choleric temperament—a child who will have great zest for life and who, when any activity is forward, will say with Bottom the Weaver 'Let me play the lion too.' The other child, however, who trips lightly on his toes as though the touch of the ground were distasteful, will be of a more thoughtful type, probably of the melancholic temperament. For the foot, too, like almost every part of the body, is a picture in miniature of the whole man; and in the foot the toe is more specially connected with the head. The heel, as has been said, expresses the activity of will, while the instep and arch of the foot manifest the power of feeling. The writer has a vivid memory of sitting in a college garden when a beautiful Indian lady walked across the grass accompanied by some lady students of the intellectual type which, among women, has now almost exclusive admittance to the higher seats of learning. The contrast between their walk and the graceful, rhythmical rise and fall of the Indian lady's step and carriage was an epitome of the contrast between two civilisations based on fundamentally different powers of the soul. So should the Goddess advance on to the stage when in the Masque of the Tempest her approach has been heralded with 'Here comes Juno, I know her by her gait!'

It is not, however, only the limbs which are the basis of the will; the metabolism plays its part as well. Most people have felt that sense of weakening in the lower organs which accompanies fear. The great virtue and vice of the will—courage and fear—have plainly much to do with metabolism. 'He has no stomach for the fight,' is more than a mere metaphor, as every frightened soldier will testify. As systems of movement, too, the limbs and the metabolism are closely connected. The movement of the heart will continue almost irrespective of limb movement; but metabolism is sure to become sluggish without a certain amount of exercise.

Between the head-nerve system and the system of limbs and metabolism there intervenes another system which takes in physical organic life the same mediating position which feeling holds between thinking and willing in the life of the soul. This is the rhythmical system, whose centre lies in the chest where the heart and lungs are situated, but which also permeates the entire organism in the pulse of the blood and the fine response of the body to the intake and the outflow of the breath. It is not difficult to see that these rhythmical processes are in reality the basis of human feeling. Whenever we feel any deep emotion, anger, or pity, or great hope or anxiety, there is sure to be an answering response in the quickening of the breath or the beating of the heart. Indeed this connection is so plain to anyone who cares to observe it that the sense of it could only have been lost to-day through that complete pre-occupation with the intellectual consciousness of the head-nerve system which is the basis of modern civilisation.*

In the rhythmic system also we find organically expressed that quality of movement which has already been alluded to in connection with the power of feeling. The rhythmic system never tires. The limbs will go no further at the end of a mere day's walk; the brain becomes

* Coleridge's *Aids to Reflection* contains an interesting division of man into head, pectoral and abdominal systems, the pectoral being described as ' at once a bridge and a barrier ' between the other two systems.

17

exhausted with a few hours' concentrated thinking; but the heart and lungs must pulse and stir without rest by day or night from the first intake of mortal air to the last out-breathing of the breath of life. It is due to this tirelessness of the rhythmic system that all work is less fatiguing in proportion as it is done rhythmically and, being so done, rests on the rhythmic system of the body. The old customs of singing and chanting at work were based on this knowledge, and students of fatigue in modern times have only rediscovered the importance of making movements rhythmical if they are not to tire. But because the connection of the rhythmic system with the power of feeling is not understood, people have not begun to study the effect of feeling on the nature of fatigue. In education, we find that intellectual work tires the children, and then, to give them relief, we exercise the opposite pole of the body by introducing violent games and sports, which exhaust them in another way. But we do not have the imagination to think that if we taught them artistically and with feeling, that is rhythmically, they would not become so tired in the first place, and so would not need violent outlets for their energies in another direction in the second. For the true experience of life through the power of feeling based on the rhythmic system is to-day at its nadir. The marvels of the universe come pat to our children without the wonder and reverence which lasted even as late as the science of the nineteenth century. And the rhythmic system has not nowadays much more chance of expressing itself through physical movement than through the movement of the soul. When Nausicaa and her maidens came to the sandy beach of Phæacia to wash their clothes they brought a ball with them with which they played a graceful singing game. Modern young maidens kick a soft football spasmodically and with raucous voices about the beach. And our soldiers are taught to perform the simplest movements in a series of arbitrary jerks more suited to robots than to men. It is the starving of the rhythmic system which has produced the modern violent dance movements and beat groups.

It should be one of the practical ideals of education to see that when a child comes to leave school he has been enabled to develop the three powers of thought, feeling, and will; and owing to the connection of these powers with the three systems of the body such an aim demands that physical education shall support spiritual development, and spiritual development shall rest on the right physical basis. This connection of the physical and spiritual elements in life, so little appreciated in modern science, is of paramount importance for the child, who is only slowly developing the physical basis on which his spiritual powers can rest. For the adult has the bodily basis matured for all the powers of his soul, even though education and environment may have stunted him in one system or another. But the child is not a little adult. His whole constitution, physical and spiritual, is different; he passes through many stages before attaining the full possibilities of manhood. But only when the goal is seen can we proceed to discuss the means of reaching it. It was first necessary to sketch the psychology of the threefold man and its relation to bodily functions. We can now proceed to examine the stages by which a child comes into possession of the powers of thought, feeling and will, and of the threefold organism on which they rest.

CHAPTER II

THE CHILD'S RELATION TO THE THREEFOLD ORGANISM AND THE THREEFOLD POWERS OF THE SOUL

When a child is born into the world he is very far from being equally perfected in all parts of his body. The head which was the first part to take form in the embryo is astonishingly large and complete; and of the head that part which is essentially head, the forehead and upper head, is far and away the most developed. For in the head too there is a part representative of the rhythmic system—the nose—and a part representative of the metabolic system—the jaw— and these parts of the head are comparatively stunted in the newly born child. This comparative height and breadth of forehead helps to give the young child's face that look of marvellous profundity which can almost overwhelm anyone who suddenly observes a child seriously setting about some piece of childish business.

The limbs on the other hand are unformed in the extreme. It is many months before they become sufficiently straightened and strengthened even to try to bear the weight of the body. Even when the child comes to be free in his running and walking they seem quite inadequate to the great head which they have to bear. For a long time in fact the child remains top-heavy. A small child asked the writer one day, ' Do you often fall over?' and suddenly made him realise that to experience his childhood again he would have to imagine that in the course of the next walk he might several times feel the sting of the ground on nose and forehead and outstretched palms. In the first few months of life the child really resembles a tadpole with its large head and the attenuated body and limbs which hang from it. The resemblance is preserved in the walk or run of the small child. The adult walks in such a way that you feel the limbs carrying the body and head; but when a child runs towards you, the head, all eagerness, appears to float towards you and the limbs to patter along in the endeavour to keep pace with the head.

The rhythmic system of the young child is also undeveloped. If you listen to his breathing when asleep it is astonishingly irregular compared with the steady ebb and flow of the sleeping adult. Indeed the small child has to be taught the habit of rhythm. Night and day are as nothing to him in the first months of his life, and he is prepared to be just as wakeful at two o'clock in the morning as at the hours which his parents consider more desirable for conscious life. He wants his food also at quite irregular times and has to be disciplined into the habits of feeding. Like the breathing, the pulse is irregular and far quicker than with adults, and the temperature in illness rises and falls in a convulsive way. The walk, too, is very spasmodic, and nothing of that springing rhythmical step characteristic of later childhood appears in the first years of life.

One process to be traced in childhood therefore is the process by which the three bodily systems become formed and completed. Like all living processes this process is a rhythmical one, and in its broader lines will be found to take place in a rhythm of seven years. By the end of the seventh year the changing of the milk teeth shows that the head is to a large extent moulded and completed, and it is from that time that the movements of a child become more and more rhythmical. A child of seven or eight perched on a high seat will almost invariably swing his legs to and fro; he will delight in the running of a stick along evenly spaced railings; the exercise in which most town children indulge of walking to school on the cracks or in the spaces of the paving-stones is another example of the truly organic desire to express the developing rhythmical system of the body.

Then comes puberty, and with it a startling change in the bodily development. The natural rhythm of the middle period of childhood often disappears. Both boys and girls, the former more especially, become for a time ungainly; their feet and hands are awkward as though too big for them. To see children of sixteen acting on a stage side by side with grown men and women is to appreciate the difference between the finished completed limb of the adult and

23

the immature still forming limb of the adolescent. The digestion too at this age begins to move towards adult desires. The great sweet-eating epoch is past, and saltier appetites begin to reign.

This process of the formation of the body in rhythms of approximately seven years is remarkably well illustrated by the development of the face itself which, in the forehead, nose and jaw is an epitome of the whole threefold man. It will be observed how little the upper part of the head has to grow after the first seven years, while the nose and jaw develop at much later periods of life. A small child with a lantern jaw is happily against nature.

As far as physical development is concerned, therefore, childhood is an age when the formative processes of the body work from the head downwards, first to the rhythmic system and then finally to the system of the limbs and metabolism. In its fullness this forming of the body is not complete until the child reaches the end of the third seven year period, that is until the twenty-first year, the traditional age for the infant to become the man. It is really more correct to say that a child ' grows down ' than that he ' grows up.'

It might be imagined from the direction of the formative process that the faculties of the soul would follow the same course as physical development, and that therefore the first mode of experience in the child would be the intellectual consciousness which depends on the head system. In actual fact, however, the reverse is the case. There is another process of development which proceeds in the opposite direction. This process is that of being awake and alive in the use of an organ, no matter how imperfectly formed. If a word for this process could be coined it might be called the process of ' awakeness '; and it must be placed in its natural contrast with the stream of physical completion.

The newly born child, though so highly perfected in the head, begins first of all to be awake in the movements of his limbs. He lies in his cot kicking his legs into straightness and moving his helpless arms spasmodically in the air. All the first elements of consciousness are bound up with limb movement. When a child of four says ' Let me see ' it is useless to hold the desired object before him to be inspected merely by the sense perception of the eye. He desires to take the object, and handle it, and make it move and work. ' Let me see with my hands ' is his real meaning. So said a small child exasperated by the adult point of view that he ' could see quite well from where he was.'

The child is in fact asleep and deeply dreaming in the experience of the head during the first six or seven years of life, and all his conscious experience is bound up with the system of movement. Watch the development of his speech and you will see how it arises from the movements of the limbs. A sentence which an adult would speak quite passively comes from the small child accompanied by a swinging of the arms, an upheaval of the whole body, or a jump into the air. Nor is the content of a child's speech meditated before it assails the ear. On the contrary, the whole charm of small children's talk is its complete inconsequence. They will say something and contradict it the next moment. Take down all their talk for the space of ten minutes, read it through to look for the meaning when the insistent presence of the speaker is gone, and you will be astonished at its utter inconsequence. But the chaotic way in which picture succeeds picture, idea melts into idea, can remind you of one sphere of your own adult consciousness. When you dream, one image melts into another in the same extravagant and seemingly chaotic manner. The adult, however, dreams in his sleep; the child whose head system is not yet awakened dreams also during the day when he appears to be awake.

The fact that little children first begin to be awake in the limb system means that the first power of the soul to be born in them is the power of the will. The will of small children is astonishing. In persistence to obtain what they want they can outdo any adult. Indeed it is not an uncommon spectacle to see a household completely dominated by the will of its youngest member. This will, however, is something which connects a child in the most direct and immediate way with the objects in his world. It leads him to imitate everything which goes on around him. If you have a child of three or four about you when you are doing a job of carpentering you need a double set of tools. When you hammer, he must hammer too; when you saw, sawing's the thing; when you chisel, chiselling is the staff of life. In fact the foundation for the whole life of will is laid during the first six or seven years of life. Happy is the child who is left free to imitate during this time and who is surrounded by activities worthy of imitation. For it is one of the sad effects of modern civilisation that it supplies so few activities for the child to copy which are really strengthening for the will. Contrast for example a child of the last century playing at coachman with a modern child playing at motor cars. The former cracked his whip, tugged manfully at the reins, shouted at the horses—all lusty activities of the will; the latter clasps a stick for a wheel, and while he sits still in his chair copies the noises of the engine and gears, and the strident tones of the klaxon. It needs little imagination to perceive that the latter is comparatively a nervous activity, even though it may call for some slight movements of the limbs. For it must not be forgotten that the hand, being also an epitome of the whole threefold man, can be used as an instrument of thought or feeling or will. A watch-maker *thinks* with his hands; a painter, through the more rhythmical movement of the wrist, uses the hand as an instrument of feeling; a blacksmith smiting the shoe on the anvil forges his hand into an instrument of the will. Civilisation, however, has not merely worked negatively with children by withdrawing from them so many healthy activities to copy; it has also positively provided them with all manner of toys—mechanical toys of the ever popular Meccano type, etc.—which definitely encourage them to develop intellectual thought at an early age through manipulation with the hands.

Those children, however, will have the best start in life who are left to develop their will through imitation during the first six or seven years of life.* For even the faculty of *feeling* is not truly born till about this age. A small child's feeling will indeed lead him to put his arms round his mother's neck and cling to her when she kisses him good-night. But the feeling is in reality a kind of organic need. For when the mother, perhaps for the first time, goes away from him, and in her absence is constantly thinking of his welfare, she is almost certain to receive a letter from the friend left in charge to say that the child is perfectly well and has not once asked after his mother. If she is tempted to call him heartless she is perhaps more right than she means to be. For the feeling life is not yet truly born—it is bound up with the organic functions. A child may even pine physically for lack of the mother whom he ' never once asked after '; conversely, to be surrounded with love is the best basis for physical health.

One way to discover at what period children begin to experience life more through the power of feeling is to see what kind of stories satisfy

* There is a type of child who keeps the faculty of imitation too late in life. Such children have an astonishing faculty for mimicry —the degeneracy of true imitation—but are often backward in the faculties of intellectual thought, etc., which should have developed later.

them at different ages. It is astonishing with how simple a story a child of four or five will be satisfied. A farmer who goes into his farmyard and feeds the animals in turn, a little duck who swims down the stream and sees the trees, bridges, boats, etc. Such simple stories, which have no plot and no development and are not much more than mere lists of natural objects, will be found entirely satisfying to such young children. Their minds are still so objective, their delight in mere things is still so strong, that the names alone are enough; the story in fact is only an extension of the child's own habit, when he first began to speak, of exclaiming the newly learnt names of all the things he sees. It is like a reminiscence of the time when the first man gave the names to all creatures of creation and 'whatsoever Adam called each thing that was the name thereof.'

But with children of seven or eight the matter is quite otherwise. You cannot come to them with such primeval stories. They need something which is still a mystery to the five year olds, the swing of the soul life between the extremes of joy and sorrow, pity and fear, laughter and sadness. There must be a moment in the story when the prince is lost in the wood and it is growing very dark; another when the light is perceived shining through the massed tree trunks; another when there comes no answer to the fearful knock on the cottage door. Such feelings on which these older children feed unconsciously are not natural to the younger ones who do not yet separate the imaginative from the real world. They will even be frightened by the more imaginative stories which are far better reserved for a later age. But with the birth of feeling the children begin to enjoy a certain measure of fear. Like the Homeric heroes they ' take their fill of sweet sadness ' and enjoy their tears. The moral life also begins to have meaning for them. They have great delight when the wicked witch is pushed in her own oven, or when the step-mother is trapped into proposing her own terrible punishment. But to children under about six the very words right and wrong are little more than names. The writer was once foolish enough to say to a small boy of four years old: ' You must not do that—it's wrong.' ' I like wrong ' was the classic reply of the child blissfully guileless of Milton's Satan.

The feeling life developing in children from the seventh year onward is naturally vastly different from the personal life of feeling in the adult. It is still closely bound to the will. In his swing between sympathy and antipathy, likes and dislikes, he expresses by bodily movements and grimaces what the adult has learnt to hide behind the mask of an immobile face. But just as in the first period of life all forms of consciousness tended to take on the colouring of the will, so now thought and will assume the characteristics of feeling. The man of feeling— the artist—will always express his thoughts in the form of pictures. Not only the professional artist but everyone of any artistic sense yearns after finding the best pictures for his thoughts.

In doing so he looks back to an earlier form of human consciousness when men thought in pictures alone, when mythology stood in the place of science, when words were alive with concrete pictorial force, and abstract terms and abstract thinking were not born. The poet tries to restore and recreate the picture content in words; the artist to give back the power of vision to human sight. The children, however, still live in the world where these things are theirs by nature and not by effort. Therefore it is that you find their *feeling* quality at its strongest if you come to them with something drawn from the older experience of mankind, with a fairy story. When you tell a fairy story to a group of children you can see that they live in your words with a depth of concentration which has passed away from the experience of the adult. As you tell the story you feel that the constantly changing pictures and the variety of moods are the very breath of life to the children. Those who do not get such things are starved of their natural food, stifled for want of their essential air.

Up to the age of six or seven the child's thinking has been immediately connected with what is physically present. Every parent has practised devices for distracting the child's attention while some object which the child covets but cannot have is removed from the field of vision and hence also from the field of consciousness. 'Out of sight, out of mind' is the natural and proper law of young children. The new independent thinking, which can follow a connected story about imaginary objects and persons, has not only the characteristic already described, that it is essentially a picture thinking. It begins to be independent of bodily vision and bodily processes but it is not independent in the same sense as adult thinking is independent. The child's natural relation to knowledge is that of question and answer. He puts the question and has an implicit belief that the adult can give the answer. Of course if a manifestly foolish answer is given he will not accept it. But the desire of his nature is to be given a right answer and so receive his knowledge at the hands of the adult. Children of three or four will ask questions and very freely contradict the answer they receive—indeed the way they treat the answers shows that the question is put more to provoke the adult to speak than in the desire for information.* But this is far from the case with children past the seventh year. There is hardly anything in life more touching than the implicit faith in such a child that his father can answer all the questions which he may put. By nature he no more doubts his father's or mother's omniscience than he questions their social position and importance in the world. The little Jean Christophe thinks his mother the most important person in the house when he goes to visit the mansion to which she has been summoned to help the servants in the kitchen.

This acceptance of authority is another consequence of the fact that the child's experience,

* This is also the view of Piaget.

his awareness, has now ascended from the limbs to the rhythmic system where it manifests itself as the power of feeling. Feeling demands rhythmical exchange between the persons it relates together. It brings them naturally into the relation of the artist and his audience where the interchange is of a subtle kind. The child is ready to give his respect and reverence; in return, he looks for counsel and wisdom.

It is only when children begin to pit their own opinions and judgements seriously against the opinions and judgements they hear that the true birth of the power of thinking takes place. This occurs about the time of puberty when the ascending stream of consciousness has reached as far as the head. Then is the true beginning of intellectual thought. It is by no means always a beautiful period. Children of fourteen or fifteen can be critical to a degree. They exasperate their parents by insisting that their way is the best. Their elders begin to feel the hungry generations treading them down.* But this critical intellectual faculty which is born in such a crude form is a necessary entrance into modern consciousness. Its good side is a real hunger for independent knowledge, and education must take this new situation in the child's life into account. But it will hardly be able to do so unless the other faculties of the soul can be harmonised with it. For what makes thinking creative is not the thinking itself but

* Mark Twain once wrote that when he was fourteen he discovered that his father knew nothing. When he was twenty-one he was astonished how much the old man had learnt in seven years!

33

the will activity brought into the thinking. Intellectual thought is by its nature analytical and destructive and conscious. But in the process of thinking there must always be present, in a higher or lower degree, the activity of will, which is the least conscious of the faculties of the soul. When we are creative in our thinking we are not conscious in the moment of creation. We go into a kind of momentary sleep, we dream of we know not what, and suddenly the idea is born. Indeed many people conceive their most fruitful ideas out of sleep itself. The problem which found no end when they consciously struggled with it is solved in the unconscious mystery of sleep.

The will however has its physical basis in the limb system, and it will not be able to enter the thought life of the period after puberty unless it has been given freedom, exercise, and nurture in the first seven years. If the will was cramped in these younger years, if the intellectual life was too soon developed, there will always be a certain destructive quality in the thought. Modern civilisation has too often seen the spectacle of brilliantly conscious young people finding themselves with no hold on life, and no reason to prolong a useless existence.

From puberty onwards there is a true basis in the child's life for the will to enter the awakening powers of thinking. For the other process of life, opposed to consciousness, the process of forming and completing, has now reached the limb system. The limbs become, as it were, individualised, and the will itself becomes a personal will. The child who was an instrument played upon by every object in his surroundings is now a centre out of which forces proceed.

With the forming of the limbs and the awakening of the head the processes of childhood begin to reach their completion. The power of initiative is born. The child begins to become the man.

Chapter III

CONSCIOUS POWERS AND ORGANIC ACTIVITY

To most people, and it would seem to most educators, the duty of the adult towards the child is that of awakening him as quickly as possible to a mature experience of life. True, there is a bewildering amount of child psychology in the world, but this child psychology is only too often directed to finding out new ways of bringing children to do advanced things. We study the best means of teaching the young child to read, because we regard reading as an essential accomplishment in the adult; we do not study whether the young child should be taught to read at all. The whole trend of much new education is towards giving children self-government, choice of their own lessons, disposal of their own hours, etc. Such systems of education call upon children to exercise adult faculties of judgement and self-dependence only to a lesser degree and in smaller spheres than the adults themselves.

An education based on a conception of the gradually awakening threefold system cannot take this point of view. If you know good reason why Nature does not of her own process awaken a faculty of the mind till a certain age you will not feel it your task as an educator to improve on Nature and develop faculties prematurely. You can do marvels with children in the way of forced development even without much apparent immediate harm. John Stuart Mill, who learnt Latin and Greek at three and re-read the principal Greek and Latin Classics more for content than style at eleven, will remain the classic example of precocious development. But in some respects all modern children are pushed forward by the very influences of the civilisation in which they live. It is almost incredible to us to-day that Charlemagne, who had the wit to administer an empire, could never properly learn to read and write, an accomplishment which many modern children teach themselves by the time they are five or six years old. But it is not so incredible if we remember how, from books, newspapers and hoardings, print is to-day incessantly shrieking at us and at our children.

These influences which nowadays surround children and make a natural development of the child so difficult are the result of conscious thought; and conscious thought owes it to children to try to give them back something of what it has taken away from them. If educational questions are urgent to-day it is because we are being forced to do with our children consciously what was formerly left to the life of instinct. But in thinking consciously about childhood we tend to use the same modes of thought that have created the environment of our mechanised civilisation.

A child however is not merely a more complicated and delicate thing than the most complicated and delicate machine; he is a thing of a different order, and requires thinking of a different order to understand him. Conscious thinking about childhood is still crude enough compared with the old instinctive wisdom concerning children. Put side by side, on the one hand, all that has been discovered about little children by modern scientific methods of research and experiment, and on the other side—the world's nursery rhymes and fairy tales! It is the poetic genius which comes at the heart of the matter, and it is a science transformed by poetic genius which will ultimately understand childhood. But in this understanding there will be poetical modes of thought which would certainly not at present be regarded as scientific. It does not however follow that they will not be true.

To begin to explore such a knowledge in its broad outlines let us consider more deeply what lies behind the facts of the threefold development outlined in the last chapter. We have noticed as a matter of simple observation that although the head is the most highly formed part of the body at birth it is relatively the slowest part to develop what we regard as its mature function—the capacity for intellectual thought. Has the head any other function in these early years of life which prevents it from developing the capacity for conscious thought, or is it in a state of simple ineffectiveness? The answer to such a question could only be discovered by a power of vision such as was developed by Rudolf Steiner; but once given it is an answer which can be endorsed by every ordinary conscientious and sensitive thinker. It is not necessary to be able to create poetry in order to appreciate and value it.

It is a kind of law of existence that the part of an organism which is a vehicle for consciousness cannot also perform an organic function. We are not, and should not be conscious in our digestion, because the function of digestion is purely organic. When we become conscious in digestion we experience pain; which is indeed nothing else than consciousness in some part or function of our body whose natural state is unconsciousness. On the other hand the head and nerves, which are vehicles of consciousness, have in the adult no organic function to fulfil in the body. They have the purely spiritual task of mediating consciousness. But when digestive processes are too strong and mount into the head we, as adults, experience headaches and we take aspirin in order to deaden the consciousness of the misplaced organic process, not realising that we are in fact deadening other forms of consciousness as well.

With children however it is different. The head remains for the child unconscious for no other reason than that it still has an organic task to fulfil. The substances which build the body naturally proceed from the lower man— the metabolism. But the formative powers which give structure and form to the substance proceed from the head. It is the forming of the body which is the essential task in the first seven years of childhood. The formative forces of the head are absorbed in this work, which is nothing less than the complete building up of the body out of a substance different from the inherited mother substance. Engaged, as they are, in this vital organic task, these formative forces only gradually become freed for spiritual and conscious ends. There is a clear sign in the process of childhood when this task is completed. It is commonly recognised that the substance of the body is transformed in regular rhythms of about seven years. At the end of the first rhythm—about the seventh year—comes the remarkable event of the loss of the milk teeth. Every teacher of children of six or seven will be familiar with the way in which an excited child will run up with a newly extracted tooth in his hand. But not many teachers know that the event is really of greater importance even than the child himself imagines. The casting out of the teeth is the last stage in the completion of a long and delicate process. The formative forces which are unable to reform and transubstantiate the hard calcined teeth go about their task in another way. They drive out the teeth which had defied the process of transformation. It is a sign that the entire substance of the body has been recreated. From this time forward the formative forces are in a large measure released from their organic work and become transformed and spiritualised as the formative forces of human thinking. As in a fairy story the spirit imprisoned in a material form is released; the doors fly open 'as if by magic' and the child enters a new realm of spiritual experience; a true metamorphosis has taken place.

To one who can follow this metamorphosis taking place in childhood and who will place beside it the development of the threefold organism described in the last chapter, many things will become apparent which should and which should not be done in the education of young children. It is undoubtedly true that you can call upon the formative powers of young children to transform themselves into spiritual and intellectual faculties. Children of three can be taught to read; at five they can be got to write little essays even without very much apparent immediate harm. But it is quite certain that in some way or other in such a treatment the formative powers will not be able to do their organic work properly. Somewhere in the bodily organisation a weakness will be left; and the man of thirty-five or forty will not know that his chronic bad indigestion or severe nervous breakdown is traceable to some physical weakness implanted in him in the early years of his life. Moreover the whole physical man is also the basis of spiritual faculties and a lack of proper forming in the bodily organs may prove for later life to have a crippling effect also on the spiritual powers. If the limb system in the child is not properly formed—and who has not seen the palefaced, spectacled intellectual child with his weak, thin legs?—there will be no true basis for the life of the will in later life. The vitality of thought itself will suffer because the will element does not enter dynamically into the consciousness.

There is therefore first of all a negative task awaiting those who appreciate this metamorphosis in early childhood—but a negative task which the conditions of modern civilisation have made a very active and strenuous one. It is to see that as far as possible the formative forces are left to their organic task and are not called away to become the vehicles of consciousness. This means, among many other things, to resist the temptation to put into children's hands all those mechanised and constructional toys which keep them so very quiet but which are in reality a kind of embodiment of intellectualism; to remember not to answer children's questions in the terms of cause and effect in which we ordinarily think, but to exercise our long disused and hard-to-come-by powers of fantasy; to forego the desire to teach our children reading and writing and other intellectual things in order that they may be up to the standard of the children in other schools and other families; in general to have patience and to pursue the ultimate good rather than the immediate triumph.

The forces of modern civilisation, already powerfully arrayed to work on the child's nerves-and-senses system and wake him up quickly from the dreams of childhood, have received an almost overwhelming reinforcement in cinema, radio, tape-recording and above all in television. But ubiquitous as these things are today, parents and teachers should think carefully of what they are doing when they subject children, especially young children, to these influences.

We begin with what may seem a technical matter in cinema and television, but one which probably conceals the greatest potential danger to children's healthy growth and vitality. Both cinema and television purport to represent movement, and more especially the movement of living people. The movement, however, is a pure illusion, caused in the cinema by a succession of static pictures, and on television by the incredibly rapid oscillations of a point of light, which produce the illusion of movement which the viewer sees.

This movement by jerks—as it may be called —deludes the conscious mind into the belief that it is perceiving movement in flow: but it does not deceive the deeper processes of the unconscious. This may not be so important in the case of the adult, though even he may be sensitive enough to experience a quality of fatigue after a film or television viewing, no matter how interesting, which he does not feel after a play in the theatre. But in the child the unconscious is working powerfully as the force of growth, and is deeply disturbed by the shattering jerks or oscillations which cause these illusory movements. There is experimental evidence that the sleep of children is more disturbed after a visit to the cinema than after any other comparable experience. But it is the long term effect which may well prove disastrous to the adult, if his growth forces in childhood have been impaired by the inner concussion of these discontinuous movements. It is as though you were to force a child to walk in a series of violent spasms, and expect him to maintain a healthy, rhythmical life.

Television and cinema share another unhappy characteristic of the present age. In modern theories of sense-perception the senses are considered to be purely passive. The eye is regarded as a sensitive camera receiving different vibrations of light on the retina. Rudolf Steiner always attacked this one-sided view of sense-perception; for he recognised also an active element of will in sense-perception. In fact we never perceive the simplest thing, a view, a picture, a human face, without constant activity of the eye. We never see the whole view, the whole picture, the whole face at the same moment. We look first at one part, then at another; and we form our picture of the whole out of this conscious activity. And the activity includes depth as well as breadth of vision. If actual depth is not given to us, as in the case of a picture, we create it by stepping forward and backward to see it in a new focus. In a theatre, also, we see the stage in depth, and an actor speaking from the back of the stage makes an entirely different impression on us from one speaking from the footlights.

At a film, or before the television screen, however, the focus of our eye never changes. We do not look, we *stare*. The screen takes away the mobility of the eye, which in children especially should be almost its outstanding feature.

These are considerations which affect the physical life of the child, and consequently the health of the adult. But there are dangers for the child in these new inventions at every level. It is obvious that both of them, but television especially, constantly subject children to scenes of violence, passion and cruelty which are quite unsuitable for them—to say nothing of the degradation of advertising invading the home. Once television is in the common living room it is almost impossible to keep such things away from the children. But a more subtle danger comes from the habit, so early acquired, of leaving the wireless or television on and not attending to it. This breeds a habit of half attention which is extremely difficult to eradicate. To many people, and to not a few children, a background noise has become a necessity of life. School children will tell you they can only do their homework when the wireless is on. Children who are accustomed to listen to a mechanical voice without attention or respect, telling them matters of no consequence to them, soon lose their natural respect for a living voice telling them things which are important for them to hear. They switch off the one as readily as the other. There is no doubt that the modern child, bred on radio and television, cannot listen to a story, or look at a book of pictures, with the same innocent concentration which children had twenty years ago. The wireless is breeding a generation of those children who cannot listen, television of those who cannot see.

Moreover, when a child is accustomed to having everything presented to him in ready-made pictures, he loses the faculty of creating his own pictures in his own imagination, to which reference has already been made. This ability to make pictures in the mind is one of the most valuable and practical gifts which childhood can make to the life of the adult. It is the basis of the imagination which can foresee the result of any action. Without it even practical consequences are not foreseen, and wisdom has to be acquired by bitter experience. Parents should think carefully before introducing into their children's lives a mechanical device which possesses an immense fascination for children, but which tends to destroy one of the most beautiful and useful qualities of the mind.

It is not an easy problem for parents to deal with. They will rightly say that if my child does not see television at home he will go next door to see it, and we shall lose him from our home. It is really a challenge to activity. If a parent stimulates active and imaginative pursuits in his own home for his own children, his neighbour's children may well come to prefer them to the passive watching of television. Their parents may become interested in this new point of view and, from small beginnings, a new movement for the imaginative occupation of children may arise. But every situation is unique and calls for its own solution.

Television and broadcasting and tape-recording have, of course, invaded the school as well as the home. They are commonly regarded as powerful aids to quick and efficient learning. Here, however, the same considerations apply as in the home. There is the enormous difference between the mechanically produced impersonal voice of the broadcaster and the living tones of the teacher; between canned and frozen music and the vital presence of the artist; between the programme laid on at set times and the artistic forming of the experience of the day, the week, the year; between the illusory representation of nature, or industry, and the total experience of all the senses; between the imaginative painting on which the mind has time to dwell and from which it gains the impulse to create, and the incessant hurrying from scene to scene from which film and television seem unable to escape. The one is food for the soul, the other for the senses and the intellect. It is the former which education should provide above all today.

Here again there can be no absolute rules. But a school which wishes to enable its children to bring into their mature years the greatest amount of the forces of life, and the greatest depth of soul experience, will use mechanical, visual and aural aids as little and as late as possible. At every age it will have to provide a compensating force of living experience. But it can sometimes be a positive thing to say ' no ' even to the most popular and attractive contemporary trends.

CHAPTER IV

THE HEART OF CHILDHOOD

We have already noticed in the second chapter an important development in childhood about the seventh year, when the awakening process of life passes over from the limb to the rhythmic system, and children, who have hitherto been so amazingly objective to life, begin to stir in the new subjective world of feeling. They can even begin to be little sentimentalists—with animals, for instance, or with some favourite toy. We must now place side by side with this development the fact that it is at the same time—and connected with the same process of development—that the formative powers first become free spiritual powers developing thought. We now find growing powers of thought independent of action in children but a kind of thought far more permeated with feeling than is found in modern adult life. Children at this age will always ask you what is your favourite colour, your favourite flower, etc., and the neutral world where you recognise the divers beauties of all flowers and colours has no sympathy from them. But in another respect also we must not expect to find in children the same type of thinking as in the adult. We are witnessing the birth of thinking, and thinking in its proper childhood is as different from thinking in its adulthood as is the child himself from the grown up. The childhood of thinking, both in the individual and in the race is a dreaming picture thinking, a thinking where the world presents itself in always changing images. We have handed down to us from the earliest days of human consciousness not logic, philosophy, or mathematics, but myths and fairy tales. Such is also the first thinking of young children except in so far as adults make it otherwise.

We have, therefore, some first principles on which to build when children enter the stage when they can be taught by instruction, when consciousness can pass directly over to consciousness without the principle of bodily imitation intervening. What the children learn must be in picture form, it must have constant variety, and it must appeal to the child's life of feeling.

It must be in picture form. This does not mean that the children must be shown many pictures; they themselves have the power to create their own pictures in the mind's eye. Indeed to show them many pictures—especially of a detailed and finished kind—may weaken their power of fantasy. A rough sketch drawn by the teacher in the presence of the children and leaving much to the imagination is far more stimulating than a realistic photograph. To show pictures and objects to young children is a strong stimulus to sense perception, and the senses belong to that brain-nervous system, which is not yet properly awakened in the

49

natural course of childhood. To tell a fairy story about a mountain, or a fable about a bear, will awaken an appreciation of mountains and bears quite other than coloured prints of the alps or a visit to the zoo. But many of the usual subjects can be taught, even if the teacher keeps within the sphere of the child's natural picture-consciousness. Letters can be learnt as pictures which the children make for themselves, arithmetic can arise from stories as well as from the child's natural love of rhythm, even the abstraction of grammar can appear in the form of Adam naming the creatures of the earth, or the centaur teaching his pupils all the activities of men.

Then the lessons must appeal to the child's life of feeling. It is perhaps this life of feeling, this soul life, which is least understood in education to-day. We instruct our children in the class room—or in the more modern fashion we allow printed books to instruct them—and then when they are tired we send them out to play games. But between knowledge and activity lies a whole world of wonder and reverence, pity, joy, tenderness and sorrow. More important than what the children learn in a lesson is to mediate the knowledge to them so that they receive from it those constantly changing moods which are the in and out breathing of the soul. It is a sad thing if in a lesson the children have not been happy to the point of shouts of laughter and then perhaps sad even to the point of tears. To form a lesson in such a way is to make it a little work of art. The children are not as yet conscious of what is artistic and what is not; but they need all the more to be given artistic food because the desire is still, so to speak, organic. Look at the imagination of children, their make believe games, their wide-eyed love of stories, their uncontrollable desire to paint and draw, the itching of their fingers to shape and model, even if they have no better material than dirty clay from a back garden, or wax pulled fearfully from the melting wall round the candle flame. This is not to be satisfied with special rooms or special hours for artistic work. Everything they learn must be transformed into wonder and beauty, there must be no ' ordinary ' lessons. Painting, modelling, acting, rhythmical movement, these must become for these young children the very way of knowledge. If you succeed in teaching in this way, you are uniting what is nowadays divided—the forces of the head with the forces of feeling and of movement. You are strengthening the binding point of thought and feeling and will. It is one of the saddest things in education to see how the intellectualising of children deprives them of their creative powers. Many such children have been known to the writer, who had been brought to a state of some proficiency in reading and writing and the doing of sums, but who were completely at a loss when paints or clay were placed in their hands. These children will often be unable to step rhythmically in time to music. One such boy was even unable to walk up the stairs counting as he walked the number of the treads. There was already a complete divorce between the powers of thought and of will.

To make the lessons artistic will be at the same time to make them varied. As in a play the scenes contrast, so in a lesson episode must follow episode, mood change into mood. To demand too much steady concentration will be damaging to the imaginative powers which are still fleeting and glance from one picture to another. These pictorial powers are the stuff out of which later abstract thinking emerges; to damage them is ultimately to stultify even the powers of thought.

For the forces which bring continuity of consciousness in time are in this second seven years of childhood in the same position as the formative powers in the first seven years. The first experience of consciousness is almost time-less. When you were a child a day loomed before you like an eternity, or was suddenly at an end; you thought it was tea time when it was really dinner, or dinner when it was tea; your parents might have been a hundred or fifteen years old for all the difference it made to you. The same absence of the sense of time made chronology an extremely difficult art for earlier humanity. Spengler recounts a case of a Greek inscription recording a pact of peace between two States to endure so many years ' from the erection of this stone.' It is because in dream life we live in the pure picture experience even to-day that in dream time has almost no meaning. The sound of the bell entering our sleeping ears awakens a train of dream events which seem to last for hours or days, before we finally reach in consciousness the sound which evoked them.* From whence comes the ability to sustain the stream of time in consciousness—not merely to be carried, as children are, in the stream of time, but to be the bearer of time in one's intellectual thought? It is born out of musical experience. The bards who taught mankind the power of song and instrument prepared the way for the later development of conscious thought. Childhood repeats this experience in miniature. The body must first be formed musically, as well as plastically, and only then can the musical force be freed for the sphere of consciousness. This is the work of the second seven years of childhood. It begins with the building of rhythm in the human body. Children begin to walk and move rhythmically by a sheer necessity of their being. The rhythmical repetition of things of whose meaning they are not yet fully conscious —so often laughed at nowadays as ' parrot-like ' —was by no means a bad experience for children. It was at least founded on a real organic need. A body of children of seven or eight who are set counting together can be safely left alone for several minutes chained to their chairs by the magic of rhythm. By nine years the rhythmical forces have so far worked upon the body that they have almost accomplished a most important work: they have brought the rhythm of heart beat and breathing nearly into time with the normal rhythm of the adult—a rhythm

* Mr. Dunne's experiments with dreams amount to a proof that the dream life is independent of time as the intellect knows it.

53

which is attuned to the movements of the heavenly bodies, and which is the foundation of rhythmical experience in music and poetry. From this time onwards conscious musical experience grows. Out of the inward sense of rhythm—the foundation of all music—arises the first pleasure in the objective rhythm of a melody. Soon the children can sustain a part in a canon, then in free harmony, until finally they win the freedom of full musical experience. But the release of musical powers only occurs gradually as the body itself is penetrated by music. After the heart and breathing have approached the normal rhythm, the muscles become more rhythmical, then the bones, and finally by the age of puberty the musical forces are released for consciousness in the same way as the formative forces were released at the change of teeth.

When the pictorial powers of the mind have been fully penetrated by musical powers out of which is born the continuity of experience, then the time is ripe for the birth of abstract intellectual thought. Speech itself is the proof that thought arises out of the interweaving of these two elements. There is a rhythmical musical element in all living speech even to this day. But in earlier civilisations it was so strong that speech was naturally rhythmical. Metrical speech came before unmetrical, poetry before prose. But there is also in speech the picture element. The artist in words is still always trying to create concrete pictures, whether by description, or by similes, metaphors, or some new association of words which bring new light and meaning into them. But language itself is full of dead metaphors—words which were originally pictures but whose concrete content has so disappeared that we can use them as abstractions. When we say such phrases as ' I understand the doctrine of splendid isolation,' we do not feel ourselves standing under anything, we do not conceive anyone teaching us anything, we do not imagine anything shining, we have no picture of an island surrounded by water. Such a manner of speech and thought, however, is entirely necessary for intellectual thought. For intellectual thought to arise picture must become abstraction and music logical connection. It was perhaps necessary that the nation which above all others mediated the abstract thought of natural science into the world should lose for a time its capacity for music and painting. While England was laying the foundation of a technical civilisation, she lost her native painting and her native music, and for centuries when she wanted painters and musicians, she had to fetch them from abroad. Indeed the natural ability for music, which made every village a home of song and dance, the natural ability for picture which covered the church walls with frescoes, and turned common objects into shapes of beauty, both these have perished because the kind of consciousness which created them has evolved further into abstract thinking. With this abstract thinking to-day every child understands mechanical principles, and a generation of children thinks itself far wiser than its forefathers whose abilities were more instinctive and more artistic. Modern children find it extremely difficult to imagine a non-technical age.

We live in a time when the culture brought about unconsciously by a common religion, common festivals, the presence of works of art in daily frequented places, the instinctive gift for song and drama, a tradition in craftsmanship and much else of old inheritance has perished to the core and left behind only a splendid museum in which some of the exhibits are still artificially made to work. How important it is, then, to make some beginning to replace all this by a living culture of education which will give a new generation a common consciousness, while making it artistically creative and not merely critically aware of the beauties of the past. Such a culture however, can only be alive if it issues from genuine springs in the human soul, as the religion and beauty of the Middle Ages issued from the natural spring of devotion in mankind never before or since flowing in such abundance. It is especially in the age between seven and fourteen when children live most naturally by the fresh powers of the soul that the common cultural life of mankind is made or marred. Can there be an education for these years grown from such deep roots in the soul that all children can partake in it as a common inheritance? And if so, what will children learn and do, and how will they learn and do it?

Anyone who has to do with young children is struck by the universality of their interests. Children who at a later age will have an abhorrence from Euclidean geometry, when they are younger love to make forms and patterns with rulers and compasses; while those to whom history will later become a sealed book delight in the stories which they hear before such things have to be prematurely learnt in chronological order and are labelled history. The ordinary human mind is indeed much more universal than is commonly supposed: the artist who prides himself on not understanding a dynamo is generally as much a product of convention as the technician who has been taught to regard poetry and music as highbrow. Let us therefore try to take our stand on something more fundamental, and ask what the subjects children learn should do for them in the period which is the heart of childhood.

On the basis of what has already been said it will be plain that between seven and fourteen the subjects taught will help to bring the children by gentle gradation from the fairy world and their still spiritual consciousness to an understanding of the material earth—above all an artistic understanding of the material earth. *Facilis descensus Averni;* he who descends too quickly and does not pause to mark the landscape on the way will hardly reascend again even though it be in pursuit of his immortal soul.

The descent into matter—such is the theme of this central period of childhood. But in this period, as in all three periods of childhood, there are three smaller periods which mark definite stages in that descent. The first from the seventh to about the ninth year is still the pure fairy tale age—assuming that children have not been already spoilt for fairy tales and that teachers understand and believe what they are telling. All the characteristic work of this period —the writing and reading, the drawing and modelling, the little plays, even to some extent the arithmetic can arise from the fairy tales, and be imbued with a fairy tale quality. There is much nature lore in fairy tales also, and it is by their means rather than by object lessons that children should first learn to love and recognise the variety of plants and trees and animals around them. Here is ample scope for two or three years, and work which can be the foundation both of the humanities and of the sciences. Fables in the second year approach nearer than fairy tales to what is human and earthly, and (if Steiner's recommendation be followed) in the third year the stories of the Old Testament, leading man from Paradise to his path on the earth will immeasurably strengthen the children's moral forces and help them rightly to the next stage of their lives.

The curriculum in the age from about the ninth to the eleventh or twelfth year has to meet the fact that children are experiencing a heightening of their ego consciousness in the feeling life—as has been described in an earlier chapter. Fairy tales can now be succeeded by myths, in the first place by the Icelandic and Germanic myths, which contain such astonishing pictures of the birth and deeds of the human ego; the Greek myths coming later as a preparation for Greek history and the more intellectual understanding of the world which the Greeks first bestowed upon mankind. Even a subject like Grammar can be introduced in such a way that the children feel their growing human powers and human responsibilities. Let them discover (as nouns) how many things they need for their daily lives—and whence those things must come; as verbs, how little the plants and animals can do in comparison with the manifold deeds of man whose upright stature and free hands allow him alone to work for his neighbour; as adjectives, what a difference a man can make to some scene, or empty house, into which he comes, how everything can be ennobled at his touch, and what it means both to the man and to his surroundings to be able to say of the things around him *nullum tetigit quod non ornavit.** But it will be still more characteristic for this age, when children begin to experience the force of their early manhood, if the nature teaching is not of a general scientific character, but relates all aspects of living nature to man himself. There is no better introduction to this period than to study with the children the life of a farm. Let them understand how the different kingdoms of nature depend on each other in a well-balanced farm, the farmer himself bringing the harmony which man must always struggle to maintain once he has broken the crust of the earth and upset the age-old economy of nature. Let them know what the farmer must be doing at all seasons of the year. It would be good if every child could plough a furrow; but, even if this is not possible,

* Johnson's tribute to Goldsmith's writings. ' He beautified everything he touched.'

59

every child can know the joy of making a little butter by the simple process of stirring cream in a glass.

In an age when men have come to regard consciousness as fortuitous and themselves as an accident on an accidental planet, teachers—at any rate those who know better—will realise the importance of giving a human view of nature as the succeeding stage to the spiritual picture to be found in fairy tales and myths. It is here above all where Steiner's whole philosophy of life makes a unique contribution to the curriculum. As their first definite study of Nature the children can begin with the most spiritual kingdom— with man himself. Not that they should study physiology (this should come somewhat later) but they should realise what it means for man that his upright position sets his senses free from the service of the body; that his hand is liberated above all special function, being neither webbed, nor hardened into a hoof, nor purely prehensile, nor padded and clawed, but a wielder of manifold tools, a master of the delicate instruments of art, the revealer of the spirit, the bestower of the gifts of love. Then later when they come to look on the animals with the help the teacher can give them, they will the more readily see that the different creatures of the earth express in their form some special power or function which is one only among the many gifts united in the universal form of man. The mouse is all trunk, the little head sunk into alignment with the body, the legs so insignificant that it appears to glide rather than run; the teeth which serve the trunk in the head are always growing, and the mouse must always be gnawing to prevent the stoppage of the mouth by the overgrowth of the teeth. Contrast with the mouse an animal like the horse. How proudly his neck arches, the head and neck becoming like another limb, free and flexible. And how his limbs have grown! Where is his heel? He is always standing high on his toes like a dancer, or like a runner lightly touching the ground with toes and fingers, waiting for the signal to start a race. A bird on the other hand has no real legs at all. When he alights on the branch of a tree you can see that his legs are really only twigs which he has flown away with! Such fanciful and human descriptions of animals give children the right eyes for their first steady view of nature; in the realm of such ideas they can work and create themselves —they are not merely learning facts.

The kingdom of plants and trees, which may be one of the main subjects for the following year, can also be seen from an essentially human point of view. Flowers have qualities as well as stamens and pistils; the seasons bring their rainbow procession of colour; the white and yellow flowers of spring and the bright yellow-green grass of the young year, the full bright colours and the red rose of summer, the deeper tones and purple leaves of autumn. The trees reveal something of the very qualities of their timber in their form and texture.

'The birch for shafts, the sallow for the mill,
   The myrrh sweet bleeding in the bitter wound;
 The warlike beech; the ash for nothing ill;

The fruitful olive; and the platane round:
The carver holme; the maple, seldom inward
    sound.'*

To see nature in this way with the poetic eye is not only the right experience for the stage of childhood: it may become the foundation of an entirely new science of the living kingdom of the world. Even in the mid-nineteenth century, Buckle, in his History of Civilisation in England, deplored the fact that poetry and science have drifted so far apart. The seventeenth century, he says, was the age when poetry still dealt with the same world as that which men contemplated scientifically. Hence it was also the great age of bold and comprehensive scientific views which gave the men of the time a great and glorious new picture of the world. Since that epoch poetry and science have crept apart—poetry concerning itself with subjective experiences, and science with the collection of facts with no fully comprehensive theory behind them. It is not for education alone that Rudolf Steiner had shown the way to make life whole and sound again by the uniting of the twin experiences of science and art.

The third stage of this middle period of child life is the first in which there arises the need for a more impersonal and abstract view of life—and it is at this stage that the children's knowledge of the world should begin to embrace the mineral kingdom. Then they should learn some of the simpler elements of physics, mechanics, electricity, etc. It will make a great difference

* Spenser: Faerie Queen: Canto I.

however if certain principles or ways of thought are followed in the teaching. How different for children to learn first about the limestone and chalk masses of the earth as of things which were once alive—death proceeding out of life, and not life born in some inexplicable way out of dead matter. It will also make a true basis for later science if the first scientific lessons deal with the phenomena which children can observe for themselves with their own senses, and do not take them immediately into scientific theory. How many children know theoretically about the movement of the earth and planets round the sun, or the influence of the Moon on the tides: but how few know whether it is Venus, or Jupiter, or Mars that hangs serene and splendid in the evening sky; or can tell you whether the moon is waxing or waning; or at what time of the day the full moon will rise. So in all subjects the beginning will be that the children learn to observe the pure phenomena. When they learn of heat they will find out what substances will burn, and in what way; they will describe the burning of wood, of coal, of coke, of peat; they will see the different parts of a candle flame or a gas jet and discover how the flame is composed. When they learn of sound they will find out (to their great surprise) what substances best carry sound, and under what conditions; they will stretch a string on a sounding box and discover the laws of its subdivision, the proportions needed for the different intervals, the nature of its vibrations and overtones. When they learn of light they will begin with the colours in which light (itself invisible) manifests itself to the senses; they will become aware of the effect on the senses of blue, red and yellow, of the emergence of colours at the point where light and darkness meet, of the complementary colour which arises in the eye itself through gazing on its opposite, of coloured shadows and the alterations of colours through distance and changes in the medium through which they are seen. The wave theory of light (which is only theory and cannot be immediately experienced) can well wait until the children have a foundation laid in experience.

History and Literature will follow the same path and remain as long as possible in the field of concrete pictures without theories. We have already followed the path of these two subjects through the first two phases of the middle period of the child's life, when they are still united— in the first the fairy tales, and in the second the myths which can lead later into the history of the peoples to whom they belong. History in the true sense can hardly be taught until there is born in children, about the twelfth year, that sense of time which goes together with the more abstract understanding to which the science lessons begin to appeal.* From the ninth year children will eagerly listen to biographies and tales of the deeds of men, but it will not concern them that Alfred lived in one century, and Richard Lion Heart in another, or that there

* See the excellent Ministry of Education pamphlet No. 23: *Teaching History.*

were other forces than pure joy of exploration behind the voyages of Drake and Cook, or the travels of David Livingstone. When children reach the first age for connected history—about the twelfth year—the descent into modern life should be as gentle and well prepared as the descent into the mineral kingdom in the teaching of science. Some pictures from the ancient Indian, Persian and Egyptian civilisations will themselves illustrate the gradual approach of man from spiritual to material things; it is a long path from the ancient Indian, whose desire was always to escape from the earth and who went up into the high mountains to die, to the Egyptian king, with his mummified body and earthly treasures spread around him, lodged in the caverns of the rock of the earth. The story of Hellas, in which mythology passes naturally into history and pictorial consciousness leads to the first scientific concepts of the world, will come naturally in the twelfth year when the children have their first scientific lessons. In a school which is fundamentally Christian (Christian in its knowledge as well as in its morality) it will be natural to take the incarnation of Christ as the central pivotal point of human history. In the following year therefore pictures of the whole Græco-Roman civilisation and its continuance and metamorphosis under the Christian impulse will naturally be taken together. The children will see that the dear city of Cecrops becomes the citadel of the human soul; and the law which protected citizen and not the slave turns into the love which gives the rich man's cloak to the beggar. The thirteenth year is the age for the great discoveries—Cabot and Columbus and the glorious Drake bursting into the Spanish Pacific, and with them Copernicus, Brahé, Kepler making the new heaven for the new earth of the explorers. In the fourteenth the children reach the full delight in the material world, when it is fitting that history should be brought from the Renaissance to the industrial age. But here, too, the great penetration of thought into matter which has produced modern machinery begins with a revolution in man's thought about the stars and planets. Ptolemaic astronomy reckoned with the penetration of spiritual planetary influence into all kingdoms of the earth: Newton applied the earthly force of gravity to the movements of the heavenly bodies.

Such examples of the progress of the teaching in one or two spheres in this middle period of a child's life must suffice for the limits of a small general book. It must be taken as the barest indication of the way in which the child's first fresh love of knowledge can be satisfied with something more than miscellaneous facts. 'There is a knowledge of natural things,' says the heading to a chapter in Job, ' but wisdom is an excellent gift of God.' Man becomes wise by taking hold of all the powers of his soul and neglecting none. The child who has lived most intensely and most deeply in the life of feeling and imagination will be best equipped for the life of thinking to which the approach of puberty will bring him.

All that has been said cuts across the principle now established in English State Education of making the change to different types of school at the age of eleven plus—an age which has become one of the principle battlefields in modern English education. The idea which lay behind the change—that it is possible at this young age to detect and segregate different types of children for different types of school, is increasingly called in question. The original method of such selection—by examination—has also been increasingly abandoned. The movement for comprehensive schools has gained ground largely because it seems to overcome the many manifest disadvantages—social and educational—of segregating children in schools which emphatically do not carry the ' equality of esteem ' which was intended.

But there is as yet no general recognition that the older practice, still seen in the public school tradition, of changing schools in the fourteenth rather than the twelfth year, is based on a sounder psychological insight than the change at eleven plus.

There is, indeed, an important change both in body and mind at the twelfth year, which has already been briefly described. It is a change which affects even the physical body. The skeleton hardens somewhat and, being the mechanical part of man, gives a basis for the first proper understanding of the mechanical in the world. At the same time sense-perception grows more acute. Such a change is a very real event, and the years from twelve to fourteen undoubtedly mark a transition stage between childhood and adolescence. But such stages can be looked on from two points of view: either as the beginning of a new epoch or the crown of an older one. Steiner thought it of great importance to view it as the latter: to bring into this age of enhanced consciousness of the world the gifts of a younger age: to keep alive the feelings of wonder and reverence in the early scientific lessons: to convert that ability of younger children to make pictures in the mind into the faculty for accurate observation: not to deprive the children of the support of surroundings and personalities on which they have come to lean while they are still so immature: generally to aim at keeping the children young rather than to jolt them by a violent change into premature self-consciousness. He did not believe there should be no radical changes in children's experiences; but that they are only good when the inner development of the children is fully calling for them.

CHAPTER V

LIFE FORCES AND DEATH FORCES

We have become so accustomed to thinking of life as a long continuous process and death as the moment of its termination that the idea of death as a force is not easy to grasp. In something the same way the Newtonian theory of light has given rise to the belief that darkness is a non-entity, a mere absence of light; and only the imaginative mind feels it on a starless night as a force around him, palpable and mysterious.

Throughout his life, however, man is a battleground between the powers of life and death, each of which has its fortress within the domain of the body. The peculiar expression of the power of life is the substance of the blood that ' very special fluid '* which pulses in our body from our first breath to our last; the expression of the power of death is the decaying substance of the nerve. The one has the task of repairing and renovating, it is more than alive and gives of its superabundance to the other substances of the body; the other is more than dead, it is in the active process of dying which destroys even substance other than itself. But through the sacrifice of its own life it becomes

* Goethe in *Faust*.

permeable by the individual spirit, and is made the vehicle of consciousness. In the eye, for instance, or any other sense organ, we are not allowed to become conscious of the nerve precisely in order that we may be conscious of the spiritual process of vision. If we have pain in our eye, if the nerve obtrudes itself as organic physical substance, our power of sight is impaired. It is only a half truth that our senses depend on physical processes; the other half is that we should have no power of sense perception at all if physical processes were not continually overcome, and the movement necessary to life in organic matter were not brought in the nerve substance into a state of stillness and death.

We can therefore extend the description given in a previous chapter of the polarity between conscious and organic activity. We must realise that every time we awaken the powers of intellectual cognition, in which we experience ourselves at our most conscious, we are calling upon the forces of death in the body. It is the same when we use the powers of sense perception in so far as they are nervous and purely receptive. Too much conscious seeing of objects, too much showing of pictures and of films and television, too much demonstration to the senses in the Lockian belief that without them the mind is a *tabula rasa*, all this wakens in the mind those processes of nervous activity which are the bearers of intellectual thought but which will easily destroy the creative powers. In the garden of Eden two trees stood side by side—the tree of life and the tree of knowledge which was also the tree of death. Children—like the human race—must come to eat of the fruit of the tree of death, and their elders have it in their hands to give it or to withhold it. But commonly they administer the fruit without even knowing from what tree it has fallen.

The intellectualism of the present day (which has produced such vast revolutions against it in the form of mass movements of emotion and will) is so universal and takes hold of children so early and so easily that it is not a simple matter to observe the time when by the natural process of growth the intellectual faculty of abstract thought naturally emerges. A process which is so commonly forced and distorted loses its natural definition and comes to be regarded as without law. Nevertheless there is a critical moment in children's development which can be understood as the natural moment for the birth of the intellectual form of thinking. It is the time of puberty, which bears to intellectual consciousness the same relation that the change of teeth holds to the pictorial dream-like consciousness.

Ability to reproduce its kind is always the sign of maturity in an organism, and with that maturity the organism is already touched by the forces which arrest growth and ultimately destroy. The plant only produces its seed when it reaches the end of its life cycle, or the life cycle of the year. The perfection of the blossom —like all perfection—is in itself witness to the presence of death. It is the same with the animal kingdom. The young animal—puppy, kitten, lamb—reaches its puberty and at once begins to grow old. It is only in the case of man—as Rudolf Steiner has pointed out—that there is a real middle age intervening between childhood and old age. Man enjoys the middle age because to him alone it is given to use the death force as power of consciousness. On this fact depends that freedom of the spirit which is the essence of manhood. But in the law of development he is no exception to animal and plant. The natural entry of the death force into the organism coincides with the ability to reproduce. The birth of the death-born intellectual thinking is the culmination of the second seven year rhythm when the change of puberty takes place. If puberty occurs earlier today it is due to the prevailing intellectualism. The importance of puberty in a child's life is commonly not so much exaggerated as misunderstood. The physical sexual change—all important for the animal—is really the least important change at this period for the human being. It can even take place in a kind of natural half-consciousness in those children in whom the nerve sense activity has not been unduly awakened. It will be of great importance, it will attract the greatest attention to itself, in the children, in the epoch—perhaps even in the nation—most remarkable for a precocious intellectualism. The whole question of sex education has become a problem of recent years for the very reason that education has become more and more a question of producing consciousness.

72

Children are not to be taught anything they cannot understand, the ' parrot-like ' method of learning by heart is condemned, and so on. The result is that by the time they reach puberty children are far too conscious in the system of the nerves and senses. What might take place in a dream-like organic manner becomes a matter of acute and even destructive consciousness.

The reason why we are in such a great hurry to-day to make children little intellectuals is perhaps that we can hardly conceive of any other form of consciousness. Deeply rooted as we are in this comparatively modern faculty of the human mind it is an effort to appreciate that the abstract thought of intellectualism is not essential to the human mind. For the outlook of intellectualism is by no means confined to the intellectuals; it is the mentality of all ordinary people. It is what leads modern humanity to see all branches of life in terms of immediate physical cause and effect. When there is a war it makes us look for economic causes, when there is a slump for trade cycles, when there is a disease, for a germ. It is only since the Renaissance, however, that people have looked for these things. Previously men looked for spiritual influences on life. History was more in the nature of biography, famine and disease were for them the punishments of God for human sins. Men were not less noble or less intelligent because they never even put the questions which we put to all every day happenings—their works of genius are a testimony to the contrary. But the time had not yet come when the consciousness of man was to be bound up with the system of the nerves and senses. Individually they grew into maturity with artistic powers undestroyed because they remained in closer connection with the rhythmic system. The village greens resounded with folk song and dance, stone and wood and the common materials of life blossomed under their hands into shapes of beauty. There was dirt and squalor and crime in abundance; but there was no ugliness, as we know ugliness to-day, because like the younger children, people remained instinctive artists. The Renaissance came like a puberty to the human race. Men ate of the tree of knowledge which is also the tree of death and they developed that type of thought by which they investigate the physical material world. This is the abstract thought which succeeded so marvellously in its application to the inorganic world that for a long time it was supposed to have unlocked all the secrets of life. To-day, happily, people are ceasing to believe that it has unlocked them all; but they are very slow to realise that intellectualism is a key which opens very limited doors, and new keys must be forged if mankind is to make new discoveries of the nature of himself and of the world of life.

At puberty, then, we witness the emergence of those forces which for the bodily life bring about the capacity for reproduction, and for the soul life create the ability to think in those abstract forms which to-day we understand as essential to thought. It will be apparent to anyone who observes children of this age that a new quality is now born in their thinking—a quality which can even be said to make this the first true independent thinking in a child's life. The thinking of younger children is not only more fleeting and pictorial; it is, so to speak, a public objective affair and arises naturally between the child and adult in question and answer. Nothing of the nature of a problem enters into it. But the first secretive thinking whereby we look upon the world from our own private corner and criticise and judge it, arises with puberty. It brings with it the first consciousness of good and evil in the world. To many children adolescence brings the first realisation that all is not right with their home and parents, with their teachers, with the world at large. They have eaten of the tree of knowledge of good and evil. They become aware of misery and oppression in the world, of temptation and sin in themselves. And how they criticise! How opinionated they can become, how eager to use their new found powers in forming judgements about the world!

The release of these new forces of consciousness* must be understood in connection with what has already been described of the development of the threefold man. It is just at this time when the stream of 'awakeness' has reached the head and nerve system that the formative powers originally proceeding from the head

* These forces of consciousness are called by Dr. Steiner the astral forces, while the formative powers are called the etheric forces.

75

have reached as far as the limb system. Hence it is that puberty is not merely the time when the intellectual faculties awaken; it is the time when there is a great enhancement of the will. There is an element of passion and turbulence playing up into the new powers of thinking. The thinking of children of this age is by no means that passionless cold thing which is the ideal of the research worker. The fierce beings of the Renaissance—a Michael Angelo or a Benvenuto Cellini—better typify this dawn of intellectual thinking.

The age of adolescence has become a far more critical one in the present century, though we have the authority of Plato that it was not the easiest of ages even in ancient Greece. All the latent unrest of this age has come to expression in mass exhibitions by young people of apathy, destructiveness, and hysteria. It has undoubtedly been encouraged by the violence of two world wars and all which attended them, by the general revolt against authority, by the decline in religious practice and belief, by the general philosophy of a ' throw-away ' economy, and many other factors. But these can only release and encourage, they do not create the latent forces of adolescence.

On the whole much of our modern education, so far from helping the situation, has had a general tendency to make things worse. It has helped in the process of waking children up to adult consciousness at too early an age: it has failed to enrich the soul experience and to nourish the imagination on which so much can be built in the adolescent age: by segregating children into different schools and ' streams,' it has produced a terrible early sense of frustration and failure in many children: it has narrowed the adolescent's horizon by specialisation just at the time when he wants to feel himself master of the world: it has imprisoned the teacher within an examination syllabus when he most needs to develop and demonstrate his freedom: it has assiduously, by its practice if not by its precept, inculcated the doctrine that the object of learning is not wisdom but the passing of examinations as a door to a higher income bracket.

Part of the purpose of this book is to show that by their very nature, Steiner Schools are a living protest against these doctrines and practices. But a paramount question at this age is what the teacher really believes about the individuality of the children he teaches. For the fundamental search of every adolescent to-day is to find himself, and all his violence is a part of this search. He is gripped by those forces of consciousness in which the ' Fall ' of man come to their strongest expression. Ultimately he will only escape from them to the extent to which he finds his true spiritual centre or ego. But does the teacher believe in such a latent spiritual centre? If he does, his impact on the adolescent will be totally different from that of the teacher who believes man to be merely a ' higher ' animal. All right relations between human beings must begin somewhere in the realm of right thinking. The expression of the relation is a matter of particular circumstances. In general, however, the adolescent secretly longs for a 'hero,' who outwardly represents his own emerging ego. He will fix his choice on whom he will, but it will be an excellent thing if he can have something of that feeling for at least some of his teachers. This will only be possible if they, on their side, feel themselves more as companions to, than as teachers of, the adolescents, because they realise that they are now confronted with a new birth within the human being, where 'deep calleth unto deep.'

But the teachers must also see to it that the new forces of the mind do not produce a purely intellectual thinking, however clear and logical and however wide its application. For not only may thought be confined to one sphere or another, but thinking may of its own nature take on one or another character. There is thought limited to the world of dead mechanical things, and there is also dead mechanical thought. When may thinking be said to partake of the death-powers no matter to what sphere it may be applied? Broadly speaking, when it is as far as possible divorced from feeling and will —that is, when it does not accept into itself the force of resurrection by which its death nature is overcome. Death is a stage and not an end in the development of thinking.

One classical example of the difference between living and dead thinking is the contrast between the wave theory of light and Goethe's theory of colour—a subject on which Rudolf

Steiner did much work. The waves are a theory added to the phenomena perceived. Nobody ever experiences them; nobody loves them or hates them; nobody ever appreciates a picture or a stained glass window more for believing that waves of different frequency are incessantly assailing his eyeballs. Goethe's theory of colour, on the contrary, is entirely based on immediate facts of human experience, which affect the human soul in the deepest way—the appearance of light seen through different media and against different backgrounds, the feelings aroused by different colours, the answer of the senses in complementing the colours seen without. If it is objected that feelings are subjective and must therefore be excluded from science, the answer is: firstly, that theories must always remain subjective and therefore ought equally to be excluded: secondly, that it is illogical to accept the facts of sense-perception and not the facts of feeling which is also a mode of experiencing the external world: and thirdly, that if feeling, when subjective, can colour and distort the objective nature of thinking, it is equally possible for the objective quality of thinking to clarify and universalise the power of feeling. There is no reason why the child of a marriage should always possess the worst qualities of both parents. The harmony of art and science visualised by Rudolf Steiner means that within the soul there is the right marriage between feeling and thinking: the latter becomes warm, living and concrete; the former clear, subtle and objective.

A simple and more familiar example may perhaps show in what way even children can apply the mode of artistic feeling experience to what is commonly regarded as a purely scientific sphere. Children are often shown pictures of a human skeleton and a gorilla skeleton side by side, or, if they are little Londoners, they are taken to the Natural History Museum where a pair of such skeletons are displayed for the edification of a curious public. They are shown the similarities in the bones and taught that the gorilla (or something like it) was the last stage before man. But if they have a proper artistic appreciation they ought to know and feel at once (the two are one) that the gorilla skeleton is derived from the human, and not the human from the gorilla. The human skeleton is a harmony, and the gorilla skeleton is the human one played out of tune. When we hear a noble piece of music played unrhythmically on a badly-tuned instrument, we know at once that this was not the music as first conceived by the musician. When we see a cheap print of a poor copy of Leonardo's Last Supper we know that Leonardo did not perfect the print in Milan, but that the print is a travesty of the master's work. So, when we allow genuine feeling to enter our contemplation of the skeletons we become at once assured that the human skeleton is the archetypal one from which all other mammal skeletons (and not only the gorilla's) are derived. The whole house of Darwin comes toppling about our astonished ears.

What has happened? Feeling has entered the

abstract sphere of thought and given birth to an idea, which can be immediately experienced as a living force. A resurrection has been made in the place of the skull; and in that moment in which thought becomes alive it grasps what is living in the thing it contemplates, the eternal form of man as the conscious work of the Creator, and not merely the last result of an incomprehensible number and variety of mindless experiments.

CHAPTER VI

THE BIRTH OF THE EGO

Hitherto we have dealt with the powers of thought, feeling and will as *things*, discussing their nature and showing when they emerge into activity during the process of childhood. It is plain, however, that there is a difference between the forces or activities of the soul and the ego which enjoys or directs them, and binds them together as experiences common to itself. That consciousness does not imply self-consciousness is, however, a truth which many people to-day overlook. Seeing consciousness in the animal kingdom they easily fall into the error of assuming that the animal possesses also self-consciousness, thereby blurring the radical distinction between man and beast, and making easier the acceptance of theories of the natural evolution of man from the animal. But the unique possession of self-consciousness by man is not merely spiritually discernible: it is physically visible in the upright position which distinguishes him from the animal. ' Cnly the lineage of man heveth heyeste his heye heved, and standeth light with his up-right body, and beholdeth the erthes under him. But yif thou, erthely man, wexest yvel out of thy wit, this figure amonesteth thee, that axest the hevene with thy righte visage, and hast areysed thy fore-heved, to heven up a-heigh they corage; so that thy thought ne be nat y-heved ne put lowe under fote, sin that thy body is so heye areysed.'* Man alone experiences through his body the axis of the heavens by which he becomes a living spirit and not like unto the beasts which perish.

That the early consciousness of children is almost devoid of self-consciousness is shown by the nature of their speech. Beginning to speak by imitation a child calls the objects of his world by the name his elders use, and among these objects the child includes himself. Hence in his first essays in speaking he calls himself Baby, or Boy, or Robert, or whatever name his parents may give him. It is only at a certain very definite moment that he first uses the word ' I.' This word is unique in all the vocabulary which the child learns, because it is the only word which cannot be learnt by imitation. If a child learnt his speech by imitation alone he would call other people ' I ' and himself—as he does at first—by his objective name. The source of the word ' I ' is altogether different from that of other words. Its use appears when there is the first birth of the ego-consciousness. Rudolf Steiner often pointed out the high importance of this moment in life. Education must take account of this sudden ability of a child to determine himself in speech as an ego. It is interesting that Darwin's contention from language in general—that there is a steady

* Boethius, translated by Chaucer.

development in kind from animal cries to human speech—has recently been upset by Professor R. A. Wilson,* who points out that Darwin took no account of the ' central unifying principle ' to be found in human speech alone.

There are two theories of childhood which have been held more or less strongly at different periods in history. The first is the theory of original sin, so strongly advanced by our Puritan fore-fathers. According to this view a child is born into the world with a predisposition to wickedness which parents and teachers must cure, generally by the medicine of the rod. It is on the whole the fashion to-day to ridicule this conception. The other view derives perhaps from Rousseau and the Sentimentalists and looks upon childhood as a state of innocence which becomes corrupted only through the wickedness of the world the children encounter —a view which is widely favoured at the present time. It is a strange and interesting thing, and of some importance for the study of psychological history, that different ages have held such opposite opinions of the nature of children.

The truth is that there is a double nature in childhood which justifies both views. There are on the one hand the gifts and dispositions which a child has as the endowment of nature, and on the other hand all that he brings to life through the force of the incarnating ego. In the first seven year period of his life a child is endowed by nature with the instinct for imitation, which is in its nature pure altruism. To

* The Miraculous Birth of Language.

sink oneself into the motion and gestures of other people is, as a process, pure unselfishness. Giving and taking are equally natural to the child in the earliest and purest age of imitation. He hospitably offers his jammy crust to all and sundry, but once offered he holds out his hand to receive it again. He still lives by the law of spiritual things where to give is also to receive. But it will not be long after a child has begun to say 'I' that he will begin to take an almost consciously wicked delight in appropriating the toy of his younger brother. Out of the developing ego there springs a tenacious and strident self-assertion which is the opposite of the altruism of imitation. You can even observe the two principles in active opposition to each other. It is a pretty thing to watch the reluctant child drawn into some activity by the overpowering organic need of imitating what is going on around him.

The same duality appears in a later age. The free imagination of the middle period of childhood is a most blessed and beautiful thing. But it is just from about the ninth year—when children begin to *feel* their ego more strongly— that they can behave to each other with great and relentless cruelty.* Especially at this time will they form themselves into little gangs and practise all sorts of terrorism over weaker children. The sense of the ego, however, is still quite a weak thing even at this age. If you ask a child of eight or nine why he has done a

* There is an excellent description of a child realising herself as an ego in Richard Hughes' *A High Wind in Jamaica.*

certain piece of naughtiness, he will in nine cases out of ten reply ' So and so told me to do it.' The child still looks for his point of direction outside himself. Children of this age have already a basis for the life beautiful of imagination; they have no basis in action for the life noble of morality.

It imports greatly for the understanding of children to realise that they naturally live by the force of the pre-Christian ego. Their law is the law of Jehovah, of the eye for the eye and the tooth for the tooth. A child will always justify himself by claiming that the other child hit him first. The law of turning the other cheek has no meaning for him certainly until well after puberty. A child who practises forgiveness before fourteen is almost certainly a prig; a man who practises revenge is a child in the guise of maturity. This does not, of course, mean that it is right for parents to tell their children, as some fathers do their boys, to hit the other fellow back. But we have to recognise the instinctive nature of children to do so, and find the best way and the best time to educate this instinct further.

The beginning must be in the understanding of why it is that into the beautiful innocence of childhood has entered a self-consciousness which brings disharmony, and clouds and chills the warm brightness of the dawn of life. It is a tragedy which can only be understood when it is seen as the tragedy not only of childhood but of mankind as a whole. When our Puritan forefathers spoke of ' original sin ' they referred the sinfulness of man to the eating of the apple of the tree of knowledge of good and evil in the garden of Eden. No doubt they understood this deed in too literal and prosaic a fashion; but it remains an imagination of one of the greatest events in the history of human consciousness. Through the temptation of Lucifer man became self-conscious before he was fit to bear that responsibility. The ego given him by Lucifer drove him from Paradise and brought him into dis-harmony with nature. The child, in whom history epitomises itself, receives the good gifts of Nature, but receives also the Luciferic ego which can manifest itself in so crude and unlovely a form.* And what can be the harmoniser of this discord in the world except that which came to harmonise that great discord which is the rift in the world's lute? It is the Christ-Ego which redeems the Lucifer ego, *Christus verus Luciferus*. What does this redemption mean in education? It means that the noble and altruistic gifts with which Nature has endowed the human soul are taken up by the human ego and become its possession. The opposition between Nature and the ego is resolved. The law is not denied but fulfilled.

In any study of the human ego we are brought face to face with the fact that there are two aspects of the ego so fundamentally differing from each other that they may be spoken of as two separate egos. The first is the ego which is purely self-assertive and sees life always in

* Nowhere has this been more powerfully described than in William Golding's *Lord of the Flies*.

87

terms of the opposition between the self and the world; the second is the ego which takes account of other egos, which unites itself through love with the world, which loses itself in order to find itself. In the dawn of idealism in adolescence is to be found the first experience of the latter ego. Mingled with a deep intensification of the individual will—for the ego now penetrates the will and gives the first sense of true responsibility—there is much nobleness of aim to be found in the young adolescents. For the dawning altruistic ego intervenes just at a time when it seems that all the beautiful forces of early childhood are lost—the innocence, the laughter for happiness alone, the fantasy, the forgiveness through immediate forgetfulness, the sense of goodness in all things. All these have vanished and seem lost, but in truth they are awaiting the metamorphosis of a rebirth. It is a time, however, when man reaps as he has sown. Have the little children had fine healthy goings-on around them to imitate when Nature bade them copy? Have their older imaginations been fed with the nourishment of myth and saga and fairy tale? If it be so, the experience of childhood, now maturing in knowledge, can be taken hold of and transformed to inner force. Imitation can turn into sympathy, the sense of goodness into moral strength, reverence into the power of blessing others. Man is at harmony with nature because the true ego is born.

This work of transformation is in reality only part of Steiner's far-reaching conception of the ego as a *transforming agent*. To many people to-day the ego is nothing more than the focus of experiences—and it is the experiences, not the focal point, which constitute the true reality. Hence some psychologists deny the existence of the ego altogether—man becomes only a bundle of experiences. Others distinguish between different egos under a variety of names. Thus Jung postulates an *Ego* which is the centre of conscious experience, but which is overwhelmed if it allows the unconscious to approach it, and a *Self* which embraces both the conscious with its ' hard won values ' and the unconscious with its ' vitality and power.' This Self constitutes the unifying element in man. As well as conscious and unconscious it unites the male and the female principles, centre and circumference, attraction and repulsion, and all the latent polarities in man. Its symbol in dream is the Mandala, circle or square, with the self implanted in the centre point.

Steiner's view of the ego transcends all such views. It is part of man's historical evolution that in the modern age he should experience his ego as a mere focal point of experience. It is this situation which has made human freedom possible. It is the narrow door through which man has to pass to win self-consciousness. But in earlier epochs, so far from experiencing his ego as the microcosmic point within, man experienced it in the great world, the macrocosm. He looked on stars and sun and moon and the life of the world and said: ' I am that, that am I.' Or rather he would have said this, as it is said to this day in Eastern tradition, if he had then had the capacity for speaking of himself as an 'I' at all. But even then this hardly conscious ego, experienced only in a kind of dream picture, was working as a transforming agent, raising man into the erect position, endowing him with the possibilities of speech and thought, giving him a continuity of experience through conscious memory. This primeval egohood has contracted into the ego of the present day, when it may almost be said that man experiences it only negatively—he is *not* any of the things he sees in the world around him. But we should be foolish to believe that any given state of an evolving entity is its final form. Some modern scientists* have indeed recognised that the only point where evolution is still possible is in man. Steiner points to the vast possibilities of transformation which lie within the 'higher' ego—the ego which will ultimately realise itself as a fully conscious spiritual entity, a transformation affecting not only man but all nature as well.

One illustration will serve to show how far modern people are from having any thoughts at all about the human ego in childhood. Children of five years old or so not infrequently ask their parents or teachers: 'Where do I come from?' It will be found almost universally that on being asked this question the parents and teachers concerned assume that they are being asked about the fact of physical birth. Some educationists indeed hold that this is the time to tell children about sex and what they generally call

* e.g. Julian Huxley.

the ' facts of life.' In reality people assume that a child means his physical body by the word ' I,' because they themselves are quite confused and uncertain in their own thinking about the nature of the ego, its relation to the physical body, whether it existed before that body and whether it survives it after death. The little child however really wishes to be assured in some such picture as many fairy tales give of his divine origin. But only those people can answer him with a truthful heart who understand childhood not merely as the unfolding of new soul forces but as the time of the gradual incarnation of the ego descending from spiritual worlds.

CHAPTER VII

BETWEEN THE INDIVIDUAL AND THE GENERAL—THE TEMPERAMENTS

To a certain extent children, like adults, find their own education. Many people looking back even as far as their childish years will realise the immense significance that the apparently chance entry of a person, a book, a place into their life has had for their whole subsequent history. This is a matter of individual destiny; but teachers are called upon to deal with large numbers of children. How can they foster what is individual in the child, even if they have to deal with a large class?

Against the danger of treating children too much in the mass must first of all be placed the opposite danger of giving the individual child too much individual attention. With the modern small family and the interest in psychology prevalent among teachers and parents the children of this century have probably received far more individual attention than did those of the last. But it is highly doubtful if the modern age rejoices in so many strong and outstanding personalities as were to be found in the nineteenth century. The truth is that it is easily possible to pay too much attention to the child's individuality. The ego in its incarnation will often show sudden flashes of originality and character which make the adult think it more mature than it really is. It is a great temptation to encourage the child's peculiar talent beyond the bearing point of the childish ego, to meet the dawning power of reason with an adult rationality which matures the child in immaturity and makes him not the father of the man but the man himself.

Before we come from children in general to the individual child there is a whole field of differentiation which was much cultivated by all branches of human science in the middle ages, but which has since fallen into complete neglect. It is the field of the temperaments, the study of which for educational, medical and social purposes has been revived and renewed by Rudolf Steiner.

There are four outstanding temperaments, and they are found in a large variety of forms and may be recognised by a large variety of characteristics. They are not to be known by any constant factors; rather by studying and living with children of different temperaments should one acquire a sense for them in something the same way as one acquires a sense for the style of a writer or artist.

Perhaps the easiest temperament to recognise —especially in children—is the choleric. Everyone knows the stocky sturdy child, often red-haired, generally with the head set well down between the shoulders, who plants his feet strongly on the earth as though he wanted to leave their impress wherever he goes, who

93

becomes by nature the leader in every enterprise, who is not easily to be moved from his ground or cajoled out of what he wants. He is the choleric child and is of immeasurable value in a class even though he may have a liking to domineer over the other children.

Neighbour to the choleric but distinguished from him by a number of features is the sanguine child who has a great deal of the choleric's interest in life but not the same tenacity in what he does. Even more than the choleric his attention is directed outwards. He spends his life, so to speak, looking out of the window; he leaves what he begins half done, and he hardly waits for the answer to the question he has just asked. But his genuine though fleeting interest makes him a good observer of external things and he is not prone to be egoistic. He is in one way typical of childhood. For not only every individual but also every age of life has its peculiar temperament and it is the nature of childhood to be sanguine. It is often necessary to distinguish characteristics due to the temperament of age from those which are truly individual. Even choleric children are sanguine by age, and have not the tenacity which is to be expected in the adult. The true sanguine child, however, will stand out by many characteristics. His walk will have a certain airy bouncing quality, and his complexion will probably be ruddy. If he paints he will ask for one sheet of paper after another and perhaps complete three or four pictures in the time when other children have hardly finished one. His paintings will probably be fresh and clean in their colours, but they will be somewhat superficial and show signs that the child has not been much affected by each colour as he painted with it.

On the other side of the choleric temperament from the sanguine lies the melancholic, which has all that the sanguine lacks and lacks all that the sanguine has. If the sanguine is in danger of being too much given to sense impressions, the danger of the melancholic is that he is so centred in himself and in his own thoughts that he has no eye for what is going on around him. If the sanguine can give a quick and ready attention to a variety of matters as they arise, the melancholic child (or man) will still be haunted by his first interest, when externally he is supposed to have some quite different matter in hand. The melancholy Jaques still harps on the fool's seventh cause when the more sanguine Duke has long ago passed on to other matters. Far more than other children the melancholic turns over in his mind what he has seen and heard. And if he is not ready with quick answers it will be found that he not only remembers but has reflected on what he heard yesterday, last week, last year. He is full of questions, he compares and enlarges, he divines inner connections, he brings together what he hears to-day and what he learnt a year ago. It is in fact the nature of the melancholic temperament to enrich everything that it touches by the transforming power of thought.

If the melancholic and sanguine temperament stand on either side of the choleric, the phlegmatic is found at the opposite pole. There are fortunately very few phlegmatic children; for it is the temperament in which there is both the least inner and the least outer activity. There are even fewer phlegmatic children than there seem to be. For many children who appear naturally phlegmatic have in reality only been made so by the fact that they have been able to take so little genuine interest in what they have to learn and do in their lives. Here and there, however, a genuine phlegmatic child is to be found. Such a child will even sit in his place when the class goes out of the room to another lesson, and be found still passively seated on their return. Children like this bring so little attention on themselves and give so little trouble that the teacher is in danger of neglecting them. Even in thinking about the children the mind tends to dwell far longer on more interesting and original children, or on those who make trouble in the class. But these uninteresting uncreative children are the very ones about whom the teacher should think most intimately, recalling every symptom of interest and activity and preparing something in each lesson for their special benefit. Contrarily, a teacher should never allow his thoughts to be disturbed or dwell unduly on the children who give him trouble. A great deal depends on the teacher forming the right relationship to the children in his thoughts.

The phlegmatic temperament, however, has its positive as well as its negative side. It possesses a certain natural calmness with which there goes, especially but not exclusively with the girls, an admirable quality of motherliness. A phlegmatic girl will often be the one who most concerns herself with other children who have fallen down, or who have been taken ill. It is a good thing to give such a child some special task in looking after another who has some weakness or disability. But to demand such a service from an active choleric child will be as galling to the one as it will be painful to the other.

For with children it is absolutely necessary to work with the temperament and not against it. The grown up can—and should—overcome his temperament out of the force of his ego. He should be able to possess himself of the virtues of every temperament, to be in himself alone every man in his humour. But the child before the birth of the ego, does not possess, he is possessed by his temperament. One of the four elements is dominating him and he has no point of human support for fighting against it. All he can do, if he is choleric, is to let the force of fire in him burn out its excess, if he is sanguine to let the air blow itself away, until other forces can also assert their influence, and all the elements become

' So mix'd in him, that Nature might stand up.'

And say to all the world, This is a man.'

For if a child is heavily charged with temperament and does not play it out in his childhood, that temperament may well remain his master even when he becomes a man. Not a few people

97

find themselves limited and hampered in the use of even outstanding capacities by the force of an overpowering temperament.

Happily that working with the temperament in childhood which can help the adult to be master of himself so far from being a disadvantage in teaching is actually one of the greatest helps that a teacher can have. It makes the large class an advantage rather than the reverse; for in a small class there may well be a poor representation of one or the other temperament, as though in an orchestra the brass, or the wind, or the strings, were too weak for the balance of the sound. But teaching with the temperaments is an art, and in art nothing is done quickly. It may even be a matter of considerable time and observation to discover a child's true temperament. It is here therefore that the long connection, already explained from another point of view, between the children and their class teacher from the seventh to the fourteenth year is so valuable in enabling the teacher to come to a thorough knowledge of every child's temperament. It is also just in these particular school years that the temperament is strongest and the child has least capacity for working against it.

What is it then, to teach with the temperaments? In the first place it is to know what to expect of each type of child. A good teacher will never ask a deeply melancholic child, What have I just said? and blame him for inattention when he does not know; nor will be expect a sanguine child to do a long concentrated task, and chide him when inevitably, he gives in half way through; nor will he ask a phlegmatic child to enact a lion, or a sanguine a cow. Or if it is a question of musical instruments he will know which child will naturally delight to hammer on the percussion, which to ' blow out his brains upon the flute,' or which will be most charmed by the fine sustained tones of the violin.

But it is in the forming and arrangement of a lesson that the greatest delight may be experienced from a knowledge of the temperaments. When you have a story to tell you may know in advance to which children you must turn when you have an adventure to relate; or when you have to imagine the hero's thoughts and feelings in suffering or disappointment: or when scene succeeds scene on some rapid journey. In every theme and period of history there will likewise be found some aspect which appeals more to one temperament than another. Some children even before puberty, will be deeply moved by the new impulse which led so many thousands, and hundreds of thousands, of the Christians of the early centuries to dedicate their lives to solitude as hermits. They will imagine them in mountain cave, or desert cell, or in some hut on the salty sea marshes, communing with the stars and elements and wrestling with the devil within. But this is only one aspect of an impulse which was changing the face of man and of the world; and others will more delight in the stories of the Crusaders and their longing to possess the very earth on which the feet of Christ had trod—that last infirmity of noble mind which yet produced such glorious ideals amid its barbarities and something like the dawning of a new world. Some children will especially appreciate a decisive dramatic act such as that of Luther in nailing his theses to the doors at Wittenberg; others will ponder, like the peasants who first saw them, over the wood-cuts he made to contrast the life of Christ with that of his Vicar in Rome.

But it is not in human subjects alone that variety of temperament finds its play. Children have a natural instinct for the fact that man is related to the world around him in more living ways than by sense perception on the one hand and digestion on the other. They feel some extract of essential human qualities in stones, animals and plants. The flowers and birds and trees are their brothers and sisters. If you try to describe the parts of a tree to them in such a way that you are not content to portray the external appearance, but that you try to live with each part in all it suffers and does, you will soon find something which will appeal strongly to the instincts of one or another temperament. Imagine only the work of the roots; let your eye illumine the dark underground and see the constant penetration of caked and hardened clay by their unresting tentacles; the splitting asunder of rocks; the ceaseless assimilation of salts and other substances; the strain, the heaving, the tenacity, the dragging at a thousand anchors, when every leaf is a sail and the hurricane winds would drive the great ship above madly through the main of heaven. Or think of the trunk; alone, individual, unchanging; wrapped from heat and cold and all external impressions by its thick coat of bark, not touched directly by the earth nor by the heavens, but cherishing its own life within itself, living always with the memory of former years imprinted in it—contrast its unchanging, almost timeless existence with the brief and varied life of the leaves and flowers; the sudden bursting from the bud, the change of colour, the immediate response to sunlight and wind, the quivering restlessness, the whirling through the air and down the lanes in the last escape, the adventurous journey of the seeds borne afar on gliding wings, or clinging to shaggy fleeces and so riding to distant places, like Arion on the dolphin's back or Ulysses issuing from the cave of the Cyclops; or swallowed of birds and sojourning like Jonah in the Whale's belly, to be delivered once more in some distant place to light and air and the new earth in which they will grow.

There is indeed hardly any aspect of human knowledge or activity into which the question of temperament does not enter. In the art of grammar, which will be the children who delight in finding those fine distinctive words which give quality and individuality to the common names of things? Which will have special pleasure in those sums in arithmetic where numbers grow larger and larger, where the farmer promises to pay the blacksmith a farthing for the first nail, a half-penny for the second, a penny for the third —and there are eight nails on each shoe? Which will like better the poetry of the man who loved to compose walking slowly on a level path beside a sheet of still water, as Wordsworth did; and which will prefer him who shouted his verses rushing down a hillside and breaking his way through the undergrowth, as Hazlitt also records of Coleridge? Or which will like best the miraculously changing imagery of Shelly's Ode to the Skylark where picture gives birth to picture as fast as bubbles chasing each other from a child's pipe?

Sometimes to modern thinking which has no belief in the quality of number, it seems arbitrary that there should be four and not five or six or seventeen temperaments. But there is a reason for the existence of four temperaments, and the reason will at the same time throw further light on the four principles (or bodies) in man which have already been described. In the intermingling of the physical body with the etheric (the body of formative and growth forces) the astral (the body of consciousness) and the ego itself it will not always come about that the same harmony will be preserved between them. Sometimes one will predominate, sometimes the other. The physical body, abstracted from those other forces which actually in life always penetrate it, is that principle of man which is subjected to gravity, which is obedient to Newton's law of motion that it will remain at rest except so far as impressed forces cause it to move. If in a child this body predominates, he will tend to become heavy and inactive in his mind and in his movements, and consequently his temperament will be that which is most removed from the sprightliness and mobility of childhood—he will be phlegmatic. The etheric forces on the other hand are those which not only form and mould substance (the infinite variety of form in the plant kingdom, the special domain of these forces, is witness to this) but work directly contrary to and overcome the force of gravity—in fact, if, like ' gravity,' the word could be made to bear two kindred meanings, they might be called the forces of ' levity.' If therefore the etheric principle is stronger in a child he will be quick and light in the movement both of mind and body; image after image, thought after thought will form themselves in quick succession in his mind—he will possess the child's characteristic temperament, the sanguine.

Suppose, on the other hand, that the astral forces, which emerge into freedom with the intellectualising age of puberty, predominate in a child. These forces (like the ego itself) are not inherited but unite with the physical and etheric bodies at birth. It is indeed their nature to overcome and destroy the inherited forces in order that the child may attain individuality—a battle which is frequently fought out to the death (so to speak) in the typical children's illnesses. If these forces predominate in a child he will at once appear more individual. In appearance he will overcome more quickly that likeness to his parents of which the healthy child hates to be reminded. He will penetrate and conquer matter more thoroughly and tenaciously. He will be more at home in the world, and will rejoice to conquer physical obstacles and situations. He will be of the choleric temperament.

But if the ego of the child predominates, the result will be very different. For in the child the ego is still hidden within, slumbering in the enchanted castle and waiting for the kiss of maturity. While it lies there it weaves its dreams and shuns the light of day. For the childish condition, therefore, the predominance of the ego spells a melancholic temperament. But when the ego is born in the man, or being born in the youth, what had been the most inward and secretive force becomes the most external and assertive. And this change affects the whole foundation of the temperaments as far as the adult is concerned—a subject which is outside the scope of a book devoted to childhood.

CHAPTER VIII

THE FORM OF A SCHOOL

In the rich variety of people and circumstances which life presents it may well sound unreal to talk about the form of a school in general. It is of course true that every school must find out its own peculiar possibilities; nevertheless in so far as schools are founded on an understanding of children such as has been described in this book they will tend to have common characteristics. In actual practice many features are found in Rudolf Steiner Schools generally, because they satisfy the needs of the children and are found by experience to be good.

For example, when there are children under six or seven to be educated, or entertained, in some kind of Nursery Class, there will certainly be no kind of intellectual teaching—reading or writing for instance—and none of the toys and pieces of apparatus which are designed to teach a sense of design, to educate the fingers by fitting pieces of material together, etc. The foundation of the nursery class life will be activities akin to all those doings and goings on which children born in the large families and houses of former generations enjoyed by a natural right of life— the mixing and stirring and pounding in the kitchen, the bed-making up and down the house, laying the table and washing up, planting seeds and bedding out in the garden, visiting the local blacksmith, watching the carpenter and plumber and plasterer and glazier in their periodical visits of repair. These are the arts of living for young children, and the Nursery Class should try to bring all these activities to the children in a life as much resembling that of a family as may be.

There is also the imaginative side of a child's life, which will become of increasing importance as the children pass the fifth year. But even before they have free imagination for stories and the like, the children's fantasy may—or may not —be stimulated by the kind of substances they handle, and the forms which surround them. Think only of the difference between the handling of wood and of metal toys—the warm friendliness of the one, breakable but mendable, and often alterable in the process of mending; and the cold rigidity of the other, unbreakable or ruined in the breaking: or between painted wood with its flat dead surface, and wood coloured with a stain which yet allows the life-markings of the grain to show through. Or think of the modern substitute—to be found in most city nursery classes—for the old low-branched climbable tree, forking this way and that, with bulges and excrescences and holes that held the water after the rain—think of the climbing frame, gaunt, monotonous, rectangular, like the steel skeleton of a new building in miniature, a true product of the mind which thinks of children as of little chimpanzees with muscles to be exercised but has no thought of what variety and interest of form can mean to the incarnating spirit!

In the Nursery Class there will be a decided difference between the children under and those above five years old. It is a great mistake to tell imaginative stories to the young children who are content with the simplest of tales; and for whose powers of growth it is even harmful to call the unfreed imagination into play. But after five children need more fantasy to satisfy the forces of imaginative thought as they gradually become freed, and they will drink in fairy tales with the same thirsty eagerness as they drink the other nourishment of their morning milk. But tales which raise questions of good and evil, where the theme is the contrast between the good princess and the bad should still be avoided, or at least softened in the telling. For the children are still in the age of physical imitation and if the doings of the bad daughter who smashes the plates and empties the porridge on the floor are vividly described the itch to go and do likewise may well be too intolerable to resist. But the simpler fairy tales—of the Brothers Grimm for instance—can be told again and again until the children know the words so well that here and there they will join in the telling; and when told and retold they can be enacted with little puppets in a home-made puppet theatre which always gives children a wonderful sense of the mysterious; or there are books to be shown with pictures made to move by strings and little levers in which the prince really cuts the thorn hedge in two, and the cook with his ladle actually gives the boy the box on the ears he raised his arm to deliver a hundred years before. At this age, too, children will delight to dress up, and act stories themselves— always provided the acting is not of formal plays with set speeches to be learned, but free and impromptu—plays in which anything may happen, and there is no harm if domestic memories interrupt the course of the plot. Then there is also modelling and painting beginning with the time when painting with a large brush on a large sheet of paper is pure joy in colour, such as a man experiences when he paints a door, up to the five and six year old children who will already begin to paint recognisable giants and men and angels. Indeed there is a whole world to be created in a Nursery Class, and it is little wonder that Dr. Steiner thought that the leader of the little children had the most important and difficult task of all; for on the kind of life she creates for the children will depend their future life of will and power of imagination. When Robert Owen, socialist, educational reformer, and general world regenerator, opened the model school for the children of his work-people in New Lanark, he caused considerable astonishment by choosing as the teacher of the little children an old weaving operative who could scarcely read or write, but who loved children and had a natural gift for finding out things that delighted them; and who had learned much patience at home from an ill-tempered and managing wife. He was entirely right in his choice; for what is wanted for these little children is not a teacher in the ordinary sense, but someone who has genius to help them to find right and rich activity, and devotion to stand aside and let them enjoy their powers. These are rare gifts and instinct alone will hardly supply them in the present age.

With the seventh year however—that is with the change of teeth—the freeing of the formative forces for mental activity brings about a quite new relation between the child and the adult. The child for the first time requires a teacher who can answer his spoken and unspoken questions about life, and who can satisfy the now conscious demand of, What shall I do? It is at this point that there is to be found something quite unique in the arrangement of Rudolf Steiner Schools. The children—who can only be properly said to enter the School at this time —on the first day of the School year meet someone who will have great influence on their lives— their class teacher. It is an important meeting; for he (or she) will go with them for seven or eight years through the school, will teach them most of what they must learn as knowledge, and will have an oversight over all that they do and are until they reach the age of puberty. There are many reasons for this arrangement which would require a whole book to deal with adequately. Perhaps the most fundamental is the fact which has already been approached from a different point of view, that children of this age do not experience knowledge as something separated into departments or abstracted from man himself; knowledge is for them a unity, and that unity is expressed in a person. It is also part of the rhythmical interplay in this age of rhythm that the child should give confidence and receive authority, and it is right that before the age of abstract thinking dawns authority should be for the child a person and not a series of impersonal rules, or the contrasting habits of diverse teachers. Many people remember far into later life the terrible sense of oppression which came over their young souls when they were presented with a list of abstract school rules; and all teachers know that when they have to take a strange class of younger children the least departure from what their usual teacher does gives real pain and creates great difficulty for the children. It is useless to say 'I am not Miss Smith' when the children's nature demands that you should not deviate by a hair's breadth from her sacred tradition.

The class teacher with his children and seven years before him can make that unity of knowledge which children desire. The fairy tales or myths he told one year he can call to life again in the children's minds, when later he comes to need them for purposes of history or geography. He must try to be something of an artist too; for in the course of lessons on nature, or science, or history there will surely arise matters that will call for painting or modelling, or a small play must be written and acted. Artistic things must arise from what the children experience in their actual lessons; they should never feel that ' art ' is a special subject with a special teacher. It is of the greatest advantage again that a teacher should come to know his children so well that he can form something of a small community of them, helping them to help each other, anticipating their difficulties, understanding their temperaments. It can be of great importance for a child's life that he should play some particular part in some particular drama—be it the angry king or surly princess in a fairy tale play, or King Arthur, or Joan of Arc, or Falstaff, or Caliban—whatever it may be—if that special experience in the immediate form which acting alone can give is right for that special child. All this can be prepared carefully beforehand by the class teacher because there has been time for an understanding of the children to grow, and freedom to form the year's work to be of benefit to one and all.

In all this work, however, the class teacher is immeasurably helped by an arrangement of the day's work, which is another important characteristic of Rudolf Steiner Schools, and by which every day itself becomes an expression of the powers of the three-fold human being. It is the most natural order for children's work—adults have forces by which they can overcome nature—if they carry out such intellectual work as they have to do when they are freshest first thing in the morning. Anyone who is really sensitive to the progress of the day will shrink from giving children mathematics or other intellectual work in the afternoon, or last thing in the morning when they are already becoming tired. But all work is not equally tiring. Rhythmical work is even a refreshment after a spell of head work. Therefore the early morning head work should be succeeded by work which calls the rhythmic system strongly into play, such lessons as flute-playing, Eurythmy, or languages in which there can be much poetry, singing, or singing games. Then in the afternoon, or late morning, hand-work, woodwork, or gymnastics give exercise and skill to the limb system. And for the younger children—at any rate under twelve—there should be no intellectual homework to exhaust the head-nerve system, and spoil the quality and depth of the children's sleep. For it is in their sleep that the real aim of education is attained—what has been consciously learned is transformed, and worked upon, and changed into capacity. How little we remember of all that we learned at school!—and how fortunate it is that we remember so little! For if every time we had to do a money sum we were to recall every process of the arabian digits, of the rule of multi-plying, dividing, etc. and how we learnt them, we should be completely paralysed, and unable to carry through the smallest transaction. Yet we do not commonly realise what an important part our sleep played in converting this painfully acquired conscious knowledge into intuitive ability.

Another thing about the first morning lesson while the children are still fresh is that the lesson need not be short. It is the practice in most Rudolf Steiner schools for the first lesson to last nearly two hours, and for this lesson in an unfail-ing daily rhythm the children come together with their class teacher. Why is forty minutes—or even half an hour—commonly found the longest possible time for a single lesson? Because the children become tired and are not able to concentrate. But why do they become tired? Because the teaching has appealed only to the intellectual understanding, and not to what is rhythmical, what has feeling, what has movement and will. But to know a thing by your head is to know it only by one-third of you; children, above all, must experience and express a thing in rhythm and movement before they can be said to know it at all. All lessons therefore, and especially the first long main lesson should be a miniature of the whole day, which is an epitome of the whole man. If a lesson proceeds from conscious learning to rhythm and activity there will be no question even of the younger children becoming tired in the two hours. But the children should become deeply engaged in what they are doing with all their powers of thought, feeling and will, and to become deeply engaged in anything means that you must have time to spread yourself in it. It is therefore far better to take the same subject day after day for three, four, or five weeks, and then allow it to rest—in order that what has been learnt may pass into forgetfulness and become capacity. Children themselves naturally follow this principle in their private interests. When Yo-yo, or stamp-collecting, or conkers or gliders are ' on,' all else is forgotten—for four or five weeks, one lives in a fever of strings, or gum, or paper and scissors, while the passion is hot. Then with startling suddenness the favourite is deposed, the joy of weeks lies abandoned on the upper shelf, a new

113

love has been found. But how different it is for teacher and children if they know that for several weeks the first two hours of every day (and perhaps more as well) will be spent in studying some period of history. There will be poems to be learned, pictures to be painted, music to be heard or played, perhaps visits to buildings, perhaps a play to see or do. Or if the subject is mathematics, how different from the first six sums in Exercise VII, it is to take, say, the cost of a house (or anything which has connection with the year's work) and work out the building costs with current rates of labour and materials—a work, perhaps of weeks, abounding in diverse interest for different types of children.

Experience shows that children who have grown up with a class teacher believe quite naturally that he can teach them all they need to know. But he on his side must always be striving to acquire new capacities and new knowledge. People sometimes ask, What about the child who cannot get on with some particular teacher? But this question does not arise with someone who is really striving to develop himself. Children always respect what has life and growth and motion; it is the static and limited in the adult which they instinctively dislike.

There is an art in the care of children's lives which is in sad need of revival. It is the art of finding appropriate ways of making conscious in them the stages of their own growth. Growth is not always slow and gradual; it sometimes proceeds by lightning leaps. There are certain moments round which it crystallises, and which it is excellent to bring to external form. You do not suddenly become a fully responsible adult—but your twenty-first birthday is an important event in that process, and rightly celebrated may help you to make something of a leap in your growth. The initiation and other rites of ancient times for children at different stages of their growth, the change of clothing, the alterations in address—the change in French and German, from the *tu* and *du* to the *vous* and *sie*—all such formalities and ceremonies brought about a conscious sense of growth and development. There is no change in children's lives more important for them than the change of puberty. It will be something exceptionally good for them if there comes a moment in this age when they are treated by adults in quite a new way—especially if this new way emphasises what is in reality the most important side of puberty—not the sexual maturity but the birth of the critical intellectual faculty. The age of fourteen, the conclusion of the second seven year rhythm of life, is therefore a fitting time for the children to say a conscious farewell to their class teacher, and to experience a variety of specialist teachers who will enjoy, one after the other, the same consecutive daily lessons for four or five weeks which the class teacher was able to devote to the different subjects. To meet a succession of personalities and to have time to enter fully into their ways and style of thought in the sphere where each is most at home and most valuable is in itself an immense strengthening of the critical powers at the point where critical ability is not negative, but instinct with appreciation and enthusiasm. But to arouse this appreciation and enthusiasm the specialist teacher must be free to decide what must be done with each group of children as he meets them—for every class is astonishingly different from the one that came before. He must be under no compulsion from examination syllabuses, or any body or person who arranges education for children in general, and not for each group of children with each individual teacher. He must decide how much group work and how much individual work is necessary; what aspects of the subject he teaches will be the best for single children and for the whole group; what amount of practical and artistic work should be included in the course; and so on. In how many different ways, for instance, one may deal with the French Revolution! Pictorially, introducing the children to such masterly historical sketches as the Flight to Varennes and other parts of Carlyle's French Revolution; economically and politically, examining the conditions of land tenure, the nature of the Estates, the difficulty of centralised government, etc.; philosophically, discovering the first appearance of the belief in the ' rights of man,' and of government as a social contract, and the influence of these theories in England, America and France—there are a dozen different ways of approaching the subject, and one or other will be the best way for each particular group. It will therefore be of the greatest help that the specialist teacher shall already know the children while they are still in the hands of the class teacher. If there is a break in the children's school life, if they go from a preparatory school to a quite separate public school, there is an enormous loss of time and energy and nervous power in the new start which has to be made, in finding out and being found out. But in a school which comprises all ages of children, the teacher of the older children will have heard them discussed in the weekly meetings of the teachers, will have seen them performing their plays and songs and other work in the periodical assemblies of the school, will have met both the children and their parents on many occasions, and will already feel himself intimate with them before he teaches them at all. Such things should be part of the natural social life of a school.

Above all, however, the effect on the children of a succession of specialised teachers will be of the greatest value if something takes place which can perhaps only be found in a Rudolf Steiner School. In ordinary teaching (whether at School or University) there is no fundamental agreement among the teachers, who in their lack of unity merely reflect the chaos of opinions which passes for knowledge in the modern world. Children are introduced to the poets, and the teacher of literature endeavours to awaken in them a love and reverence for poetry. They read perhaps the *Ancient Mariner*, or Wordsworth's *Ode on the Intimations of Immorality*, or Shelley's *Prometheus Unbound*, but in what they learn about nature in their scientific lessons, the fundamental thought in these great works would be represented as the purest nonsense—if indeed it ever entered the heads of the teachers of these subjects to mention such matters at all. It is pure superstition to think that the killing of an albatross could affect the weather; everyone knows that children are produced biologically by the conjunction of the male and female, and do not exist before that event; and as for the idea that human love could affect processes in nature, could melt the cold of the poles, and unprison the spellbound vegetative forces of the moon— well, natural science has not yet detected and measured any influence of human love on the growth of a single blade of grass. So there remain two classes of subject—those which have human and cultural value, and those which tell you the truth about the world. The best you can do in the end with this situation is to tell the children that there are independent spheres of life, the sphere of knowledge, the sphere of art, the sphere of morality, but that although each has its own values, they do not interpenetrate or affect each other.

Whether or no these contradictions become or are made apparent to children wrestling with their first intellectual experience after puberty, or whether they remain as a half-conscious background to their life, one thing is certain. At a time when they most want to be founded and secured in knowledge, this incoherence produces a weakness in the children's souls whose consequence it is difficult later to escape. It may even produce a generation reconciled to ignorance and incurious on fundamental things of life—the immortality of the soul, the problem of good and evil, the destiny of the earth. But if every teacher confirms the other, because together they have attained to a knowledge which unites art and science and religion, what a strengthening there is for the child's powers of soul at this critical time of his life! Such a knowledge is the anthroposophy of Rudolf Steiner, uniting the man of science with the man of art and the man of religion. The children have heard, perhaps in a religion lesson, of how the peoples of the East still preserve from ancient times the desire to escape from the earth—to meditate until they pass into Nirvana, and finally to escape altogether from the wheel of rebirth; while from the West—from America especially the great centre of sub-earthly electrical forces— comes the impulse to be hardened in earth experience, to conquer the forces of the earth and to realise the earthly personality which is to be gained in so doing. In a lesson on natural science they may study the characteristic food stuffs of the earth; rice in the East—sown in the water, so little earthly is it in its nature, with the seeds spread out at the end of the stem as though already scattering into the heavens: and in the West, maize with its hard cob shell close down to the dry hard earth from which it grows. Then they will hear in History of the corn lands of the Mediterranean peoples, the corn, whose fruit is neither diffuse in form like the rice, nor hardened and encrusted like the maize, but keeps the balance between the two. They will hear of how the Greek people felt that life lay in the middle way, and their great philosophers gave birth to the doctrine of the mean—man walking between Scylla and Charybdis, the good ever threatened by the two extremes of evil; and of One who also walked in Mediterranean lands, who said I am the Bread of Life and was crucified in the middle between two thieves. All forms of experience may thus unite to create a common human science, a knowledge of man which unites him as a spiritual being with the forces of nature.

One aspect of school life tends to be taken somewhat for granted in Rudolf Steiner Schools —the principal of co-education. This is perhaps because the emphasis is laid on a more important form of co-education—the co-education of art and science—generally kept in such monastic separation alike in schools and in the world at large.* But it is both natural and inevitable that an education which aims at developing a balance in life should wish to educate boys and girls together. Briefly it may be said that the female sex represents the tendency not to be sufficiently incarnated in the body ,while the male sex tends towards too deep a penetration into physical matter. Hence girls are by general nature more spiritual and religious and artistic, more malleable under educational influences, not experiencing so deeply the materialism of puberty, and entering earlier into the idealism of youth. It is, however, just because of the difference in the sexes that co-education is valuable, at any rate when the spiritual difference between the sexes is understood. It is of the greatest advantage to

* Cf. C. P. Snow's *Two Worlds*.

be able to balance the quicker, more intuitive, and sometimes more superficial intelligence of the girls with the slower and more solid and observant understanding of the boys. In an external way co-education is already something like a marriage of art and science. And the two sexes can not only impart some of their natural virtues each to the other; they can help to cure each other's vices. For while boys—by themselves—indulge more in physical brutality, girls are equally guilty of such spiritual cruelty as spitefulness. Rightly managed, the association of the two sexes can help to cure both of their weaknesses. But this can perhaps only satisfactorily be done in an artistic education, and particularly in one where the artistic sense penetrates the domain of science.

Then it must not be forgotten that co-education of the children will lead naturally to co-operation of men and women as their teachers. There is something terribly arid and unreal in a staff of women teachers only, or exclusively of men with some wives in a dubious position in the background. A natural co-operation of men and women has a most healthy effect on the children who experience it. And when all is said no education which aims at developing the spirit in man can base itself on a separation of the two sexes.

Allusion has already been made to the weekly meeting of the teachers to discuss the children and the work of the School in general. These Rudolf Steiner regarded as the heart of the entire work, for in them the teachers learn from each other, and discover how to carry a common responsibility.

Chapter IX

EDUCATION AND SOCIETY*

There is much talk to-day about education for a new society, and there is no doubt that education has brought about many important social changes. It is plain, however, that it is impossible to educate for a new social order without some idea of what that social order should be, and it is commonly a pernicious form of education which puts in the forefront the ideal of moulding the next generation into some prescribed social form. The real object of education should be to leave the next generation in the best possible condition to create its own social forms. The father who wants his son to be better than he is will help his son most by trying to be as good as he can himself—not by throwing over his own life as hopeless and planning things better for his son. An educational philosophy which is full of hope for the next generation but has nothing to offer for the immediate experience and practice of life in its own time is like a man who tries to train others in a skill he has never aspired to practise himself. Rudolf Steiner had a great contribution to make to the subject of

---

* The reader should remember that this was written in 1940. Postscripts at the end of the chapter bring the matter to the present time.

education largely because he entered so deeply into the immediate social, economic and cultural question of his day.

The relation of the individual to society is something which must vitally affect education. The Liberal State had it as its practice, if not as its theory, that you must educate the individual and leave society to look after itself; the totalitarian State holds both in theory and practice that you must train the individual for the State and the State alone.* The only view which can possibly reconcile these two conflicting claims is one which sees that for a harmony to exist between individual and State the one must be a reflection of the other:—or, rather, the powers through which the individual ego expresses itself must also work on the formation of society, so that both will be a reflection—or incarnation—of the same spiritual forces. As human history is the story of the incarnation of the ego, the relation between individual and state has undergone many profound changes. When Plato wanted to examine the nature of justice he had to build a picture of the State in order to advance from that to the individual soul—and the final justice for the individual, which depends on the laws of reincarnation and destiny, could only be alluded to in a myth at the end of the Republic. When Rudolf Steiner entered upon the consideration of Society he began with the threefold powers of the soul and showed how these same powers are

* The announcement of the suppression of Rudolf Steiner Schools in Germany by the Nazi regime frankly stated that these Schools encouraged the development of the individual.

striving to assert themselves in modern society. For a Society which does not, in our present age recognise that man has become an individual ego is merely a relapse into former conditions of life when individual freedom had no meaning for the majority of mankind.

Unhappily in the present century Europe experienced a very serious relapse in this respect. The Liberal Idealism which seemed to have been gathering more and more strength during the nineteenth century was for a time pretty well exterminated in most countries of Europe, and is now on a highly precarious basis. Rudolf Steiner was perhaps the only person in Europe who was already alive to the coming danger during the first World War and who pointed out clearly that a complete revision of the principles of Society was necessary to avoid it. This was nothing less than a conscious recognition of principles which had been trying in a confused way to establish themselves since the Renaissance, and the very confusion of which was leading mankind to disaster.

Man is related to his fellow men in three different ways. Firstly, he shares in the common spiritual experience of his age; he follows this or that religion; he agrees or disagrees with his neighbour on this or that scientific theory, or ethical standard; he is devoted to literature, art, or music. This aspect of life, which may be called generally the spiritual life, has been the centre of a long and severe struggle since the Reformation. The results of the struggle may be summarised by saying that—until the advent of the totalitarian State—the old doctrine *cuius regio eius religio* had given place to the belief in freedom of thought, which in the first aspect of the struggle commonly meant freedom of religious thought. The spiritual life is the only sphere where the liberty of the individual can be essentially found.

Secondly, man is associated with his fellow men on a basis where each one shares in a community of rights. It is now universally agreed in theory that a man should not be allowed to starve because a new invention takes his work away from him, or because he loses a limb under a motor-car. He receives an unemployment allowance, or is awarded compensation by a jury, as the case may be. A man's right to the goods he needs for his life, however, is represented by his income, and by an old tradition his income is generally in the form of wages for actual labour he performs. But human labour enters into the life of economics as a commodity. Its value depends on supply or demand, and the warmth of a man's clothing or the nourishment of his children depend on the state of the labour market and not on the amount of cloth and bread available for use. Such things are known and recognised as unjust and illogical by everybody. Few people, however, realise that such a fundamental ' right ' as a man's income should not be determined in the economic sphere at all.* The function of the economic sphere is to produce—

* This is least of all recognised by the Socialist party, whose ideal is ' full employment ' in order to put the necessary means of living in the pockets of the workers.

125

this and nothing else. All questions of human rights should be determined in a special ' rights ' sphere, where people stand on the equal basis of their own humanity, no matter what their occupation or abilities. Not that there should be absolute equality between man and man, for all men and all occupations do not require equal conditions; though there are spheres, such as the Law, in which all men should be completely equal. In practice, the political State has been compelled more and more to interfere in the question of the individual's income, and so divorce it from the sphere of his labour. Income Tax, Unemployment and Health Insurance, Old Age Pensions, Workmen's Compensation, etc., are nothing more than a clumsy and expensive way of establishing such a ' Rights ' State by little pieces. Each one in a fragmentary way aims at some other basis for a man's income than the so-called economic value of his work.

But it will also be agreed that, thirdly, a man must to some extent be related to his fellow-men as a producer in one sphere or another; and for the majority this must be directly in the economic sphere. The conditions of modern industrial life, however, not only demand the united labour of the hands in a single factory; they demand the united labour of men all over the world. Industry is to-day the great teacher of brotherhood, and economic autarchy merely one of the complications of the disease called the totalitarian State. During the nineteenth century there was a natural tendency for the production of goods to depend more and more on the co-operation of all parts of the earth, corresponding to the natural tendency towards independent freedom in the spiritual life. Industry might be, and commonly was, pursued by the single capitalist for the most selfish reasons; but in itself it was something which brought an essential fraternal and co-operative influence into the life of mankind. Every child was taught that the whole earth had to be brought together to furnish his breakfast table; and this had been very far from the case a few centuries before when his little ancestor rose in the morning to swill down his home-made bread and home-cured bacon with his quart of home-brewed ale.

There are therefore three essential spheres in human society, and the health of each of them (and hence of society as a whole) depends on its fulfilling its peculiar law, and realising its peculiar virtue. There is the spiritual sphere, under the sign of liberty; the rights sphere under the sign of equality; and the economic sphere, under the sign of fraternity. The first is the sphere of the individual the second the sphere of the social organisation or nation, the third is the sphere of the whole earth. Nothing fruitful is born in the spiritual sphere when individual freedom is denied; nothing fruitful comes into the economic life which prevents the association of all parts of the earth; nothing fruitful enters the social life which neglects the common rights of individuals and denies the special political genius of each group or nation in maintaining those rights.

Rudolf Steiner however most earnestly pointed

out that the time had come for a complete separation of the three spheres of life. Indeed the independence of the spiritual sphere from the political, virtually recognised in all liberal countries before the first Great War, could perhaps only have been maintained and extended if those countries had taken the further step and recognised that the time had come for the political State to abandon its authority over the economic life as well. In human affairs there is either progress or retrogression; in the long run nothing is conserved by pure conservatism. Such an abandonment is no doubt a difficult step for the political nation to take; but it is not more difficult, nor more destructive of nationality, than was the abandonment of the nation's claim to determine the religion and censor the thoughts of the individual. It may well take as long a struggle to bring about the former, as it took to accomplish the latter. It is perhaps chiefly on that struggle that the world has been unconsciously engaged.

This book is not concerned with describing the proposals Rudolf Steiner made for the three-fold State in general; it must confine itself to the spiritual sphere in which education essentially stands. And first it will be evident that education will be successful and achieve its real aims to the extent to which it is able to live under the sign of the spiritual sphere of which it is a part—the sign of liberty. Steiner made a kind of pattern or emblem for this when he called the first school he created the *Free* Waldorf School —free from direction by the political State.

Freedom naturally implies responsibility and an understanding of the task undertaken. Such responsibility and understanding can be recognised in a group no less than an individual. A group of responsible and free individuals with a balance of attainments and experience is the only form in which freedom can be fully realised in education. It should therefore be the aim of all people concerned in the spiritual life to make the birth of such groups possible. There is no other way of ensuring the continuance of free creative power in the educational life of mankind.

One most important consequence of recognising the place of education in the spiritual sphere is that the demands society is entitled to make on education become clearly defined. In earlier times the divisions of human life were represented by actual divisions of human beings —castes or social orders into which a man was more or less irrevocably born. To-day every single man is a member of all three spheres of the social order. Piers Plowman is no longer content with his ploughing but must find his own way to the Tower of Truth, nor can scholars be cloistered from civic responsibilities or the economic basis of life. It follows therefore that the spiritual life can no longer educate for itself as it did in the Middle Ages; it must take into account the fact that the individual to-day stands in all three spheres of life, and the economic and rights spheres have some demand to make of the spiritual sphere in the matter of educating the next generation of their members. It will be plain, however, that the demands made by the spheres of rights and economy on education cannot contravene the essential character of liberty which belongs to the spiritual sphere. The Rights State may demand that a child should be taught or helped to become a social being in general; but it cannot demand that he shall be trained for any particular form of social order. The Economic State may demand that a child shall be trained to be skilful both in hand and head as far as may be; it cannot demand that he shall be prepared for any particular profession or occupation. It may be very good educationally for a child or group of children to learn how to mend boots, as a training in skill or a help in the development of character; but it is not the task of a school to make cobblers. On the contrary the interests both of individual and society are best served when education takes as its model what nature has done with the human form itself, withdrawing it from all specialisation of function, and so leaving it free to enter into any or all.

Both individual development and changes in economic life demand more and more that a man shall be versatile. A clerk may discover that his real work lies on the land; new inventions kill old forms of industry and create new—there must be a basis of general adaptability on which to meet such inner and outer changes. There will no doubt be children who develop some special talent which requires exceptional attention and practice, children with a gift for music or languages or mechanical construction. Such a gift will certainly profit by finding some balance in other aspects of education, however greatly it may seem to demand specialisation. But in itself, too, it must be developed on a broad basis and for its own sake, and there is a certain universality in all things when so pursued. The man may become a car mechanic, or a foreign representative, or a bridge designer, or an accountant, but it would be a gross interference with his freedom to train him as such when a child. At school he must study mathematics or languages, or mechanical principles for their own sake and for the sake of the development of his own understanding and character, not to fit him for one particular task in the economic and social life. Educators can only claim the right to be free themselves if they jealously guard the freedom of those they educate.

Finally, this freedom of the spiritual life must be expressed in its whole relation with other aspects of life. We are so accustomed to a world in which ' he who pays the piper calls the tune,' that we forget there would be no tunes if pipers had not once been free to make them. Actually the economic life is continually receiving free gifts from the spiritual life. Every time industry uses trigonometry, the differential calculus, the pulley, the lever, the laws of expansion, gravity, social unions, the principles of contract and so on, it stands indebted to the spiritual life for its magnificent former achievements. It is a debt industry never pays and never is asked to pay; for the spiritual life does not make loans and advances; it gives free gifts. But the spiritual life cannot continue to make these free gifts unless it receives free unconditional gifts in return. The very money which enters the spiritual sphere should follow a different law from that which is used in industry. It should be gift money; and this gift money should be renewed as freely as man himself is renewed out of the powers of his spiritual life. For the life of the spirit is ultimately the only guarantee of the continuance even of the life of industry; because, as Rudolf Steiner once said, you may feed a single man with bread, but you can only feed a community by giving it an understanding of the world.

Postscript to the second edition (1942)

Since this book was written, a good many new tendencies have shown themselves in the sphere of education, on which it may not be out of place to add some comment. The first and greatest is the enormous advance of opinion towards the socialisation of education and the bringing of all schools within the framework of the State.

Anyone who examines the arguments brought forward by those who advocate this reconstruction, and is sensitive to the tone which lies behind them, will be struck by the fact that they are chiefly concerned with the social and economic advantages which are said to be enjoyed by those who have been educated in independent schools. What is in itself a purely educational question is transferred to social and economic spheres. But supposing we could keep the question in the purely educational sphere and ask simply: ' Is it better for this child to be educated in a Secondary School, or a Public School, or—shall we say—a Rudolf Steiner School? '—then we should first have to decide to whom the question should be put. For in such immediate concrete cases we are at once brought up against the contradiction, which Rudolf Steiner often pointed out, between Socialism and Democracy. Socialism would say: This question must be put to the State and the State must decide what type of education it will provide, allowing perhaps for some experimental schools on sufferance. Democracy would say: The object of Society being to secure the maximum amount of freedom for the individual, this question must be put to the parent, who is responsible for his child and therefore has the right to send him to what school he pleases.

If we take the democratic point of view and ask the parents it is obvious that we shall get a variety of answers but that the answers will be practically conditioned by the financial circumstances of the parents. Some will be free to send their children to the school of their choice, others will not. Here is a manifest inequality which is genuinely felt to be an injustice. The Socialist solution is to abolish the inequality by driving every child into the State School. But there is another solution, equally equalitarian and more truly in accord with British individualistic tradition—namely, to extend to all the privileges now possessed by the few, to make it possible for all parents to choose, and therefore to have sympathy with, the schools to which they send their children. As along ago as 1855 Disraeli wrote:—

' The basis of English society is equality. But here let us distinguish: there are two kinds of equality; there is the equality that levels and destroys, and the equality that elevates and creates. It is this last, this sublime, this celestial equality, that animates the laws of England. The principle of the first equality, base, terrestrial, Gallic and grovelling, is that no one should be privileged: the principle of English equality is that everyone should be privileged.'

We are already very far advanced into the Socialist state, and it will not of course be possible suddenly to establish all schools on a freer basis. But it is possible tentatively to suggest a means by which a beginning might be made. The education of children costs the State or public authority x pounds a year for each child. That means that the individual is entitled if he chooses to x pounds' worth of educational services each year for each of his children. It will cost the public purse no more for the State to say to the individual: If you choose to send your child to a non-State school which has justified itself by reaching a certain size and, existing for a certain number of years, we will pay an equivalent (or possibly a somewhat smaller) sum of money for his education in that school, as we have ourselves been relieved from the expense of educating him.* I believe that if this could be done an enormous number of people, who at present have to send their children to State schools, would wish to co-operate with an equally large number of teachers who would be eager to found such free schools. In some districts it would come about that the free schools would absorb the State Schools; in others they would continue to exist side by side; in others there might be at first no impulse for a free school at all. But the interest in, and enthusiasm for, education for its own sake would be everywhere immeasurably enhanced. For the individual would be exercising the equality of privilege—he would be more a man and less a unit within the State.

The objections that will be at once raised to such a scheme are only a little more obvious than their refutation. Two things in especial will no doubt be said: that the State cannot provide the money for work it does not control, and that we shall have a chaos of conflicting standards and practices in education. To the first it may be replied that the State does not provide the money for anything—it merely collects it from individuals in the form of taxes, and redistributes it in payments. It is therefore the individual who provides the cash who should have the maximum influence in deciding its application, particularly in what closely concerns himself.

* This is not quite the same as the ' free gifts ' from industry to the spiritual life described in *The Threefold State*, but a step towards it.

The other objection is based on fear of freedom and distrust of the ordinary citizen's good sense ——the same fear and the same distrust which has always tried to suppress liberty of thought. The citizen does not dress extravagantly or preposterously because he is left free to choose his own clothes, and he can equally be relied on to choose a sensible school for his children as a sensible coat for his back. It would be an excellent thing if, in the plans for reconstruction after the war, provision were made for one such free School—not limited by economic causes, as at present, to the middle and upper classes—in every fair-sized community. Nor is there any reason why there should not be a central council of such free Schools to discuss common problems and adjust common difficulties. But such a council would naturally be entirely divorced from the political state.

One significant feature of the proposed unification of education is that, in attempting to abolish one form of class distinction, you may in reality substitute another and an even more terrible one. For it is an integral part of the whole idea that there should be different schools for children of different abilities and capacities. You would thus have (as you have already to a large extent in state schools) a class system based on supposed ability instead of on social tradition or money. This is the efficiency view of education: it is assuredly not the spiritual view, or the civic view. It would immeasurably increase that gulf between the more highly and less highly educated which is such a distressing feature of modern life and has led to the dreadful categories ' high-brow ' and ' low-brow.' Already the gulf between public school and state school is being rivalled by the gulf between secondary school and elementary school.* A division of life based on intellectual intelligence is perhaps the worst from which any community can suffer.

For the children also it would have very adverse effects. Intelligence is not always born at the precise moment when educators would like to detect and classify it—witness our present Prime Minister† who first began to exercise his mind at a time and in a station where most men have abandoned that thankless operation—as a subaltern in the regular army. Both parents and teachers, however, would naturally wish their children to proceed to the higher schools and the shadow of the competitive examination would fall upon children's lives even more heavily than it does at present, when Elementary Schools must receive their children with a certain knowledge already forced in to them in the Nursery Schools, because they in their turn have to look forward to the demands of the Secondary Schools. This skimming of the cream from each school has also socially the most undesirable effects. Nothing is more salutary for a school than the presence in it of a small body of gifted older children enthusiastically pursuing their studies for their own sake; and perhaps nothing is more salutary for such a body of children than

* Now (1967) between grammar and modern school.
† i.e. Winston Churchill.

137

to live and work among less gifted children whom they must learn to appreciate, whom they can help, and from whom they probably have much to learn.*

In the Waldorf School—which was a kind of pattern for all schools in the modern age— Steiner set his face against all such divisions and separations, including the class division. Children of all abilities learnt together—and even in the higher classes where there was naturally more specialisation, certain common cultural subjects, which are the language between man and man, were studied together as the common inheritance of all mankind. Even children who would commonly have been regarded as defective and sent to special schools were given special lessons in a ' helping ' class and spent part of the day with their more fortunate fellows. And rich and poor, aristocrat and plebeian, sent their children together to the School, not because they were forced to do so by the Almighty State, but because they regarded it as the best School they knew of. They were exercising the equality, not of regimentation, but of privilege.

Postscript to the third edition (1952)

It may fairly be claimed that the prophecy of the above postscript has been broadly fulfilled by

* Some modern research reveals that ' streaming ' is not good even for the most gifted children.

the operation of the new Butler Education Act. The attainment of Grammar School status at the age of eleven has become so enormously important in a child's life that young children often suffer immensely from nervous strain in these formative years. At the same time from the side of the independent schools—especially the public schools—all of which face ultimate extinction from economic pressure, a demand has arisen for help from the State for individual pupils along the lines indicated. In a recent correspondence in *The Times* (1952) Mr. Robert Birley suggested income-tax relief for parents sending their children to approved independent schools, Sir Cyril Norwood advocated a grant for each child. In the leader which summed up this correspondence, *The Times* declared both schemes impractical, because a Socialist Government would never agree to either, and therefore the independent schools would become the shuttlecock of contending political factions. This is, of course, a purely political point of view, which has nothing to do with education, and is a prime example of the intrusion of the political into the educational sphere, where it does not belong. *The Times*' solution for the survival of the independent (Public) Schools is that they should increasingly become schools for children sent to them by the local education Authority. This means, on the one hand, that the schools would gradually lose their freedom, and, on the other that fewer and fewer parents would be able to exercise any right of choice of school for their children. A section in the Butler Act encourages local Authorities to help parents to send children to the school of their choice. In practice it has proved almost impossible to persuade local Authorities to do so.

Postscript to the fourth edition (1967)

The years since the last edition of this book have witnessed some encouraging developments in education. The status (and pay) of teachers has been greatly raised: the place of the arts in education has been fully established and much valuable work is now being done: the dangers of premature specialisation are at least recognised: the training colleges for teachers are very different from thirty years ago. The segregation of children into different schools at 11+ is widely regarded as a mistake, and the examination for that purpose is virtually abandoned. The Socialist solution to the difficulties it has occasioned is the Comprehensive School, which is widely different from the comprehensive schooling advocated by Rudolf Steiner, and means the extinction of many well established traditional schools. But the fundamental question of the relation of schools to the State remains a battle in which those who wish to maintain the independence of the old traditional schools seem to be steadily losing ground. The question asked by the Labour Government is: How can independent schools be integrated in the State system? It is never asked: How can State Schools achieve a greater measure of independence?

One noteworthy attempt to carry the battle into the other camp, has, however, been made in a remarkably able book *Education and the State** by Dr. E. G. West. In a fully documented examination of the history of education Dr. West demolishes the generally accepted myth that the lower classes were illiterate until the Forster Act established State Schools in 1870. He believes it would have been far better if Mr. Gladstone's advice had been followed and the State had encouraged and strengthened ' the vast amount of voluntary effort which exists throughout the country.' He attacks local authorities for not operating the Butler Education Act as it was plainly intended to be operated, by increasingly taking away from parents the freedom to choose a school for their child.

His practical proposals are very similar to those advocated in the postscript to the second edition of this book, that parents should be given ' educational vouchers ' to enable them to send their children to independent schools if they wish to do so. The book received some enthusiastic reviews in many leading journals, and the question was asked whether it represented the turning of the tide?

Meanwhile the financial position of such unendowed schools as the Steiner Schools grows increasingly difficult. In practically every other country of Europe—and notably in

* Institute of Economic Affairs. London.

Scandinavia — they receive generous help
from the State, either for capital expenditure,
or for running expenses, or both. Britain
alone opts for the equality that ' levels and
destroys.'

NOTE ON THE COVER PICTURE

This picture is attributed to Botticini (of the School of Botticelli) and is in the Uffizi Gallery in Florence. It represents the story of Tobias from the apocryphal Book of Tobit, so well known and so often painted in the Middle Ages and up to the Renaissance, but forgotten in the Protestant West which no longer includes the Books of the Apocrypha in its Bible.

The story belongs to the time of the Captivity of the Ten Tribes in Assyria. Old Tobit has fallen on evil days and has become blind. He sends his son Tobias on a journey to Media, where he has left a sum of money with a friend. The boy hires a guide in the market-place of Nineveh, who proves in the end to be none other than the Archangel Raphael. The Book tells of the adventures on the road, and of the Mystery of the Fish, caught in the Tigris, by whose virtue Tobias heals and wins his young bride and on his return cures his father's blindness.

It is a boy's journey to puberty, the way of a child, undertaken under the sign of the Fish—that sign in which the early Christians recognised 'the physician son of Mary.'

The Book of Tobit tells us only of the one Archangel, Raphael, but the genius of the painter has added two other Archangels to complete the picture of the guiding Powers of Childhood. Gabriel, the Archangel of birth and of the first years, gazes with loving devotion at the child, leaving him free to play out unimpeded his natural instincts and impulses: Michael in full armour and with sword erect marches ahead, confident that the boy will follow his hero: Raphael takes him by the hand and leads him on the road, giving his protective care and receiving loving trust and confidence.

The three figures present an image of the attitude of the teacher in the three ages of childhood which have been described in this book. The picture is a Meditation on childhood, and reveals to those who will ponder it the inner mystery of the developing powers of the soul. It is a guide and an inspiration for every teacher and parent.